# TAKING CARE
# OF PARENTS
# WHO DIDN'T TAKE
# CARE OF YOU

# Taking Care of Parents Who Didn't Take Care of You

## Making Peace with Aging Parents

### Eleanor Cade

Hazelden
Center City, Minnesota 55012-0176

1-800-328-0094
1-651-213-4590 (Fax)
www.hazelden.org

Library of Congress Cataloging-in-Publication Data

Cade, Eleanor.
    Taking care of parents who didn't take care of you : making peace with aging
parents / Eleanor Cade.
        p.  cm.
    Includes index.
    ISBN 1-56838-879-9 softcover
        1. Aging parents—Care—United States.  2. Aging parents—United States—
    Family relationships.  3. Adult children of aging parents—United States—
    Psychology.  4. Adult children of dysfunctional families—United States—
    Psychology.    I. Title.

    HQ1063.6 .C33 2002
    306.874'084'6—dc21

                                                                    2002068648

06                    6  5  4  3  2

Cover design by Theresa Gedig
Interior design by Elizabeth Cleveland
Typesetting by Stanton Publication Services, Inc.

# CONTENTS

## ACKNOWLEDGMENTS

Many people shared their caregiving experiences with me, and I thank them all. At their request, they shall remain anonymous. Their stories are true but may have been edited for clarity. Names, locations, and other identifying circumstances have been changed to protect confidentiality.

In addition, I am grateful to the following for their expertise: Clark Barshinger, Ph.D.; John Huh, M.D.; Lojan LaRowe, Ph.D.; Z. Ted Lorenc, M.D.; Elizabeth Morrison, L.C.S.W.; Moe Ross, M.Ed., Miographies; Arn Schaper, Ph.D.; Candace Sinclair, L.C.P.C.; and Linda Westphal, L.C.S.W. Any errors or misinterpretations are my own.

Doni, Julie, Kandy, Mary Linda, Mindy, Sherry, and Vickie deserve special mention for their extraordinary ability to listen, offer wise counsel, and make me laugh. My sister Linda has opened many doors for me, and I shall always be grateful. Lor, Joey, and Maria grace all who know them with their gentle spirits and kind hearts. I thank Karen Chernyaev for her editorial expertise and calm voice. I thank Coleen O'Shea for her friendship and cheerful support. Both she and Angela Miller were instrumental in bringing this book to life. Finally, I thank Davey, Dubbie, and Cakes. Their unwavering love and encouragement bring joy and freedom to my life. No embrace is more comforting than theirs.

# INTRODUCTION

In 1900, few people in the United States lived beyond age sixty-five. Today, thanks to medical technology and a high standard of living, Americans can expect to live well into their eighties. The U.S. Census Bureau tells us that thirty-five million people were over sixty-five years of age when we celebrated the millennium. By 2030, we can expect that number to jump to seventy million people, or 20 percent of the population. By 2050, it is projected that nineteen million people will be eighty-five or older.

Living longer is no guarantee of a healthy mind and body. The longer any of us live, the more likely it is that we'll be living with more than one chronic illness. It's not unusual to hear seniors comparing notes on their bad backs, failing eyesight, heart surgeries, joint replacements, and pharmacy bills. As seniors age, and their health fails, they need more and more help with the simple activities of daily living—getting dressed, preparing and eating meals, dispensing medications, maintaining personal hygiene, cleaning the house, and paying bills.

The fact is, our parents are going to be around a lot longer than any generation before them, and we will be faced with the challenges of long-term caregiving. Most of us, however, will be caregivers without the support of an extended family or the strong communities that were available to previous generations.

According to the National Alliance for Caregiving, in 1998, more than twenty-two million households were providing care to an elder—nearly triple the number of caregiving households in 1988. The typical caregiver is a forty-six-year-old woman who graduated from high school. She is married, working full time, with a median household income of $35,000 per year. She is averaging close to eighteen hours each week caring for a seventy-seven-year-old relative, but one in five caregivers devotes forty hours or more each week.

These numbers are more than just statistics. These are our parents—and us, the adult children. Caregiving means the demands on our time and energy will increase. It means that many of us will have eldercare responsibilities well into our retirement years, at a time when some of us will be dealing with the aches and pains of our own aging process. It means that we're going to need help too.

Caregiving in and of itself is difficult enough, but what if our parents weren't very good parents? What if they were difficult and dysfunctional, so much so that our relationship with them is sour and distant? What if their substance abuse or mental illness caused them to neglect us, mistreat us? There are any number of reasons why some adult children walk away from the call to care for parents, but most of us decide to stay, even when we're not sure we should have to, or even want to.

*Taking Care of Parents Who Didn't Take Care of You* is for those adult children who are in the throes of taking care of parents—difficult parents, dysfunctional parents, parents who weren't so good at parenting. It is for those of us who are exhausted, overwhelmed, and wondering if we have it in us to weather yet another family catastrophe. It's for those of us who are frustrated, scared, and running out of energy and ideas.

Although the term *caregiver* is used throughout this book, in many cases *care manager* would be a better description. This book is for anyone involved in caring for his or her parents, regardless of who is living where or with whom. The kinds of caregiving, the living arrangements, and the time spent with parents will differ from reader to reader, but this book is for those adult children who are struggling to do the best they can.

In addition to providing insight and useful information for dealing with the domestic issues of caregiving from housing to hygiene, this book is a guide to the psychological and emotional issues that arise when adult children find themselves taking care of their aging parents. It suggests that there is a developmental cycle to caregiving, one with a beginning and an end, a cycle that offers closure on the past and acceptance of the present. It offers a path to come to terms with our parents, to get beyond the paralysis, resentment, regret, and deep grief that caregivers experience. We can learn to navigate the minefields of aging parents and family dysfunctions and create new, emotionally healthy roles to replace the old family scripts.

This book includes personal accounts of other caregivers who have shared this journey. When we hear other voices, we realize we are not alone, that other adult children are struggling with some of the same issues, that other parents are difficult too, and perhaps even worse. We also hear fresh ideas worth investigating, additional sources for help, and better ways of coping as caregivers.

*Taking Care of Parents Who Didn't Take Care of You* is about more than caregiving. It's about taking care of ourselves. It's about letting go of the past and coming to terms with the present. It's about grieving over what we didn't get and learning to appreciate what we did get. It's about acceptance and making peace. It's about discovering that it's possible to do what has to be done—and to find healing in the process.

Taking care of our parents is an opportunity. We have the chance to break the cycle of our childhood experience, to let go of whatever neglect and inattention we suffered, and to begin a new era in our family's history. We can discover a gentleness within ourselves as we come to terms with old issues and choose a new role, one of compassion, caring, and love.

# I

---

# THEY'VE FALLEN AND THEY CAN'T GET UP

## OUR PARENTS NEED HELP

# ONE

## CAREGIVERS' STORIES

Margaret's parents lived hand to mouth, and much of what went in their mouths was alcohol. Margaret went to a dentist for the first time when she was old enough to work and pay for the visit herself, but it was too late to save her front teeth. She has had false teeth since she was sixteen. Now her mother is a widow, penniless, confused, unable to live alone. What should Margaret do? Does she have to take care of the woman who didn't take care of her?

Jill's father left home when she was ten, leaving his wife and children to fend for themselves. Twenty years later, he has returned because he's ailing, scared into sobriety after a recent heart attack. He has no money and is living in a welfare hotel. Jill's sister is furious and flatly refuses to see him, much less help, but Jill is torn. She doesn't know what to do.

What do we do when our parents are getting old and need our help? If we decide to care for our elderly relatives, we will face many hard choices and complex issues. But if we've had a difficult relationship with our parents all our lives, we will face other issues as well. They weren't easy to deal with when we were young, and they may be worse now. The truth is, we probably don't want to take care of them.

Even the thought of caregiving makes us angry and resentful. *They weren't there for me when I was a child,* we argue, *so why should I be there for them now?*

Yet these are our parents. We want to do the right thing, but we have a spouse, children, job, friends—our own life. What's the right thing to do? If they were lousy parents, are we supposed to drop everything and help them?

Ron's mother was angry, abusive, and had a raging temper. She yelled at Ron, chased him, hit him, called him names. Her punishments were arbitrary and severe. Now she is in her early eighties, still angry and abusive, but she is widowed, a breast-cancer survivor, and fearful about living on her own much longer. Ron worked hard to find sanity and peace in his adult life, and he fears that taking care of her will bring back the grim worldview he had as a child. Yet his mother needs help. What should Ron do?

What if the relationship between our parents and us has been extremely hard, even toxic? Are we going to be thrown back into the dysfunction of our childhood, or can we manage to be levelheaded in our dealings with them now?

Darlene's father molested her repeatedly. Although her mother feigned ignorance, there was no doubt that she knew what was happening. Years later, her mother is widowed and suffering from emphysema. She wants Darlene to return home and take care of her. Should Darlene offer protection and care to her mother? Her mother certainly didn't protect Darlene.

Mary is the youngest child. She was conceived after her parents were divorced, but because of the surprise pregnancy, they remarried. Mary's mother never forgave her, telling Mary she was unwanted, unloved, and the cause of her mother's unhappiness. Now her mother has Alzheimer's dis-

ease and is no longer able to function on her own. Mary—
the child her mother didn't want, the child she tried to
abort—is now the child that her mother turns to for help.
Mary can barely make sense of the situation, much less decide what she should do.

---

These stories are true, but what makes them moving is that
these adult children eventually did make the choice to care
for their aging parents. In spite of their childhood experiences, they became caregivers to parents who had not par-
ented them. In spite of the issues from their pasts, they chose
to treat their parents with kindness and mercy.

What is remarkable, however, is that these stories are not
unusual. Dysfunctional or not, our parents are aging and they
need help. We may not want to deal with them in their old
age, but most of us will. And we will find ourselves in one of
the most challenging situations we've ever confronted.

Make no mistake about it. Even in normal, emotionally
stable families, watching our parents age and taking care of
them is a very difficult task. "My family is functional, loving,
'healthy' by any standard. We get along, everyone cooper-
ates, and there are considerable financial resources," said
Carolyn. "But even with everything going for us, dealing with
my father's illness was dreadful."

Taking care of elderly parents is difficult enough, but taking care of parents with whom we have a host of issues is
something else. We are stepping back into a family system
that never worked well. Caretaker issues, already difficult
and stressful, are fraught with additional dilemmas, such as
control issues over money, addictions that are still rampant,

siblings who refuse to help. The list is long because the family system itself is still essentially dysfunctional. In these situations, adult children face their own family-of-origin issues yet again as they struggle to find a functional family role and make sure their parents' needs are met at the same time.

---

There is little generational precedence for today's caregiving issues. Previous generations died younger and more quickly. An extended final illness was often only a year or two. Extended family lived nearby, providing siblings, cousins, aunts, and uncles to help share the burden of an elder's care. Families were part of a large and supportive community.

Medical care is better now, however. Our parents are living longer lives, though not always healthier ones. At the same time, family members are scattered, unable to help on a regular basis if our parents suffer long, lingering illnesses and years of incapacity.

Every caregiver has a story. Each may differ in detail, but all are markedly similar in process. My story is simply one example of what many adult children face as they become caregivers to their aging parents. It is not exceptional, but typical. As the population ages, as life expectancy increases, as extended families continue to live apart, this sort of story will become far too common.

### ELEANOR'S STORY

Long after I was married and when my children were teenagers, my parents and in-laws showed signs of failing health. One by one, they became physically weaker, emotionally more needy, and mentally less capable. After some years of this, my husband and I found ourselves doing more and more for them. Like it or not, we had become the frontline care managers. We were in new, untried territory, with no one to lead us and in denial of the toll caregiving would take on our lives.

In the beginning, neither my husband nor I thought of our parents as being dysfunctional. We had our problems, yes, but those problems were "normal" to us. Only after the caregiving was in full swing did we begin to look back on some of the events in our childhoods, seeing for the first time that dysfunction existed in our families from day one. Alcohol abuse, emotional dependence, unresolved anger and conflict, undiagnosed mental illnesses, poor relational skills—all of these were part of the family dysfunction, further complicating our duties as caregivers.

Although undiagnosed for many years, it is obvious now that my mother suffered from a mild depression for most of her life. This made it very difficult for her to cope with the normal stressful life events that happen to everyone, so she was often overwhelmed and in bed, sick and depressed. My father worked long hours, using his job to escape an unhappy marriage. Unable to control my mother or his marriage, he would micromanage everyone around him. I became the family caretaker, the problem solver, the codependent, the go-between.

My eldercare journey began when my mother was in her midseventies and severely compromised from a lifetime of smoking. She wanted to move near me, the family member she trusted most, because her respiratory system was failing. My father had finally retired in his late seventies, but he was unhappy about quitting work only to become a caretaker for his wife. He was angry and resentful and wanted me to help him—or better yet, to take over. And so my parents moved across the country and settled about two miles from me. In a classic example of denial, I was certain this arrangement would work. *Once they are settled and make new friends,* I thought, *this will be fine. They'll be happy, my husband and I are close by, and the children will enjoy being near their grandparents.*

In less than four months, I had put both parents in the hospital. My mother had pneumonia, and two days after she was released from the hospital, my father suffered a debilitating stroke. Living independently was no longer an option. They needed help. Immediately.

In the beginning, I experienced a wave of confusing feelings. Old emotional scars started to hurt. I was shocked at the change in the family and the need my parents now had for me. I was angry that I was already providing care for my parents, when, in my view, they were still capable of caring for themselves. Past issues, long suppressed and ignored, now reappeared. I had to figure out what to do about my parents while balancing the conflicting interests of my teenagers and my marriage. I was plagued by self-doubt, codependence, anger, recriminations, and guilt.

I had to face my own intense resentment of the burden my parents had become. I had to face the fact that my family of origin, with its many dysfunctions, was back in my life. There was no doubt that my parents weren't going to get better, and I knew they would expect me to fulfill a longtime role of dutiful daughter. They weren't going to be realistic about their situation, and they weren't going to appreciate what I was doing.

I gave them access to my life to fill the holes in their own. But no matter how much I gave, more was expected. Not surprisingly, it wasn't long before I was exhausted, trying to make them comfortable and happy—a goal I would never achieve.

A new life challenge was beginning. Yet facing such a challenge while coping with dysfunctional family issues was overwhelming. Worse, the family issues were still building. My in-laws were aging and they had problems too, problems with addiction that were unknown to my husband and me until we were managing their care.

While my parents were living near us and requiring daily contact at some level, my in-laws' situation was deteriorating into a series of long-distance crises. My mother-in-law, now frail with osteoporosis and other ailments, was hospitalized several times for heart problems and overuse of prescription drugs. My father-in-law was showing signs of organic brain dysfunction due to years of alcohol and tranquilizer abuse. Agitated, suicidal, now living in his own mental hell, he had to be heavily medicated to ease his distress. At different times, each of them required extended nursing-home care in order to gain enough strength to return home.

Every time the phone rang, my body tensed. My husband and I were being dragged back into our families of origin—finding ourselves in the role of mission control—with not a clue as to what we should do or how we should do it. We were overwhelmed and resentful. "They're asking too much. We have a life, we have teenagers, we have jobs." We were beside ourselves. "Why us?" we raged. "It's not fair!"

But what choice did we have? They were our parents, our family. There was no place to run, no place to hide. Our siblings were unavailable, living far away and too paralyzed by their own problems and the family system to be of much assistance.

We were on a new path, one that was hard and gut

wrenching. Through trial and error, research and experience, we became experts on geriatric mental health, drug interactions, and addictions. We learned more than we wanted to know about strokes, heart disease, chronic obstructive pulmonary disease, and emergency medicine. We worked with doctors, support groups, counselors, and the healthcare system, but no matter what we did, our parents continued to become more frail, more helpless, more needy.

We made countless trips to doctors, hospitals, and airports. We sought advice from accountants, pharmacists, psychiatrists, lawyers, and other professionals, discovering along the way how to become advocates for our parents and protect their interests. We became parents to our parents, trying to preserve their independence and dignity while still seeing that they received the care and assistance they needed.

Their lives had become so difficult, and they were so sad and helpless. We found ourselves grieving while they were still alive. The grief triggered other losses, and we grieved for the family of origin we wanted and would never have. We cried over what had been wrong and what we could not change from the past. We hurt for the loss of what we did have. We wept as we watched their bodies and minds wither away.

Because neither set of parents could function on their own, we explored various living arrangements for them. The choice that seemed best for them was to create a nursing home for each set of parents—in their homes. This was a good choice financially, and it allowed each set of parents to feel that they were still independent.

For my husband and me, however, the care management continued. We still had to be constantly available for health emergencies, and there were many. We had to field anxious calls from housekeepers. There seemed to be a crisis every day: one parent was refusing to take any medication at all, another was sneaking extra doses, another was throwing a temper tantrum, another was refusing to bathe.

We regularly contacted social workers, doctors, visiting nurses, and counselors. We tracked changes in medication. We installed grab bars in showers, hired painters and roofers, kept up the routine maintenance they could no longer manage. We phoned, visited, or talked to caregivers daily, trying to keep the peace and keep the network functioning.

Stress grew to unbearable levels. Coping with the needs of parents, children, jobs, and possessions was impossible. There was no time or energy left over for each other or ourselves. Over time my body began to show the effects, but I ignored the symptoms. This, too, is fairly common among caregivers because we are so busy taking care of everyone else that we don't bother to care of ourselves. Now I was the one in the hospital, needing surgery to repair the ravages of stress. The cause, according to one doctor, was "acute neglect." This time, taking care of myself was no longer an option. It was a necessity.

But there was an unexpected change in our lives that neither my husband nor I foresaw. Caregiving had turned into a door that opened to old family issues, long unresolved. Although we were facing these issues again, this time around we were finding resolution. We were adults now, and we no longer had to react like we did when we were children. We now had psychological tools, we had choices, and we learned to exercise them. We learned how to carve out a new role for ourselves and still work within the family system. We quietly set new boundaries and started taking care of ourselves.

The surprise was the healing that occurred. It was a slow process, but we came to terms with our parents, making peace with them. Even though the caregiving continued to be demanding and challenging, we made an effort to focus on the good things they had done for us. We realized we were letting go of old resentments, accepting our parents for having done the best they knew how to do.

Although it seems that the caregiving burden will go on indefinitely, it does not. Sooner or later, bodies and minds give out, and we lose our parents to eternity. But as this was happening, we discovered new respect for our parents, admiring their tenacity, their dignity, their need to feel independent. We talked to our parents about their lives, and we listened with new compassion.

We had learned to love our parents again, even as we were saying good-bye.

---

Despite all the problems, I was fortunate to have had some lovely and peaceful moments with my parents. One night as I was putting my father in bed, he asked me to sit with him a little longer, so I pulled up a chair and turned off the light.

He began to talk about my mother, telling me about the gray hat she was wearing the first time he noticed her. She was a beautiful woman, he said, and he missed her so, and he longed to be with her once again.

He told me he loved me and was proud of me and was sorry that he was a burden. I told him I loved him too and he wasn't a burden. I held his hand, knowing that he had done the best he knew how to do and neither wanted nor intended to be a problem for me.

I kissed him on the forehead and told him he was a good father and I would miss him when he was gone.

And I knew in my heart that I was telling both of us the truth.

# TWO

---

## RETURNING TO HELP AGING PARENTS

There is no way to prepare for being a caregiver. Few of us have pondered whether we will or won't care for our parents. The idea crosses our mind fleetingly, if at all. Life moves along, and sooner or later, we find ourselves doing what needs to be done. Thinking about it comes much later.

### SURPRISE

The beginning of our caregiver journey often begins with a surprise, perhaps an accident or an unexpected medical diagnosis. Or the parent with whom we have little or no contact is now in touch and asking for assistance. There's an emergency, a crisis, and suddenly our parents need help.

If we see our parents regularly, we are probably aware that they have been slowing down lately, showing signs of mental and physical aging. Perhaps we've noticed that housekeeping chores are getting more difficult, or Mom's not acting like herself lately, or Dad seems overly concerned about the price of groceries. Still, as long as our parents are managing, we continue with our own lives, checking in occasionally and not worrying about them.

After Jimmy's father unexpectedly died, it was soon obvious that his mother was not going to be able to live by herself. "She was pretty addled," Jimmy said. "Apparently Dad had been keeping her on track for some time, but now that he was gone, she was lost."

Barbara's parents moved from California to Kentucky to be closer to her. "It was like they used their last ounce of energy to move, and when they got here, they were done. They were too frail to care for themselves anymore. They couldn't even unpack the boxes."

Patty took her mother to the doctor, concerned about what appeared to be depression. After a number of tests, the diagnosis turned out to be Parkinson's disease coupled with early signs of dementia. "I couldn't believe it. I thought she was just being contrary about taking her medicine."

John and his sisters were worried about their mother. "There were some inconsistencies in her behavior that we just couldn't ignore any longer," John said. After several doctors had completed an evaluation of her physical and mental condition, they were told Mom had Alzheimer's disease.

A heart attack, stroke, death of a spouse, broken hip, mental breakdown—situations like these catch us off guard. We're shocked, for they had been doing so well for so long. If we had thought about it at all, and we probably hadn't, a crisis with our parents was something to deal with later— maybe a few years from now. We certainly didn't expect this event to be so sudden, so catastrophic, or so soon.

## DENIAL

Denial is generally the first line of defense after any loss or trauma. In a dysfunctional family, denial is the lens through which all events are perceived.

Denial is when we say that we didn't see it coming. The signs, however, were probably there all along. Cherie said, "You can see how sick my mother was when you look at pictures from my son's high school graduation, but I didn't see it then. She looked like that all the time. The point is, she was sick all the time."

Cynthia said, "My mother had a thing about this cat— insisted she had a second cat when I knew she didn't. Still I thought, well, maybe she's feeding a stray. It was when she was looking for Dad, who had passed away several years earlier, that I started paying attention."

Denial is when we say, "Let's get them back on their feet, so that their lives can get back to normal." What we really want is for *our* lives to return to normal. *If we can just get them "fixed,"* we think, *we won't have to be so involved anymore.* We don't want to see that as soon as one problem is dealt with, the next one will appear.

"First, it was Dad's heart attack," Jerry said. "Then it was finding him a place to live near me. Then it was figuring out how to get meals for him because he couldn't cook. Then his leg started bothering him, and he was having trouble walking. It was just one thing after another."

Denial is when we think the problem is situational and it will be easy to help out for a while. "No problem," we say. What we're denying are the signals that our parents need much more, that this is the beginning of their increasing dependence on us. And we are slow to see the ripple effects that their needs will create in our lives.

To begin with, our spouse and children are drawn into the problem immediately, simply because we're less available to them. Dinner is fast food again, and maybe our teenager can help the younger ones with homework tonight. We've got to pick up a prescription for Dad, find someone to fix the gutters on his house, take Mom to physical therapy, stop by Tuesday night to make sure their bills are paid.

Our job suffers too. We need extra time off to take them to doctor appointments, we're interrupted by parental phone calls, and we're impatient with our co-workers and customers. The truth is, we're distracted and tired and impatient with everybody.

Denial is when we think we can set aside old issues and build a new relationship with our parents. We tell ourselves that things will be different this time, that our parents have changed. What we're denying is our own feelings, perhaps anger or abandonment or betrayal. We're also denying the very real possibility that nothing has changed, that our parents will be just as they always were.

Denial is when we tell ourselves that the situation is temporary, that it will soon be resolved. What we're denying is our parents' inevitable decline and a future where they'll need ongoing, permanent help. Maybe we can make the present situation more stable, but if we think about it, we know in our hearts that this is just the beginning. The situation today is about as good as it's ever going to be.

### EARLY SIGNS OF CHANGE

If we see our parents regularly, we are in a good position to recognize early signs of change. One of the ways we can tell how our parents are doing is to ask ourselves how we are feeling. If we are starting to feel a bit disturbed, even uneasy, when we are around them, it's probably for good reason. There is change is the air, something is different, though we can't quite put our finger on it. It may be subtle, beneath the surface, yet on an unconscious level, we are responding to it.

Our edginess is a signpost, a signal that we should not ignore. Our body is telling us that it's time to pay closer attention to our parents. We may not be able to put our response into words at this point, but we are responding intuitively.

If we're getting irritated and annoyed all the time, we're likely to blame ourselves. We know we should be more patient with them, less demanding. Rather than blame ourselves, we should look for the source of our negative feelings and ask ourselves what happened to cause these feelings.

It may help to start a journal. Keeping a record will help us become conscious of the changes that are occurring. Our goal is not to document who's impossible or what dumb thing he or she did. We're simply looking for changes in behavior. The question is not whether what they're doing is good or bad. The question is whether we're seeing the same old behavior, perhaps exacerbated—or something new.

Bob said, "My dad starting obsessing all the time about the traffic in town and how hard it was to make a left-hand turn. There wasn't much traffic at all, but he had figured out how to get to the post office and grocery store making only right-hand turns. It took me awhile to realize that he was losing his ability to drive and was using traffic as an excuse."

What we want to recognize is that something is changing. More often than not, early signs of needing help are there if we choose to see them. Yet most of us probably ignored these signs. It was only after we became full-blown caregivers that we could look back and see what was there all the time.

## THE CALL WE CAN'T REFUSE

The love between parent and child is precious. What we may not realize is that underneath our surprise and denial is a profound sadness. We are starting to lose the most important relationship of our lives. These are the parents who brought us into this world, and they're getting ready to leave us.

Or maybe these parents of ours weren't such good parents. They did the best they could, but we needed more love, more attention, more care than they could give us. Maybe we're still waiting and hoping for that love and attention and care, but we haven't gotten it yet . . . and now it looks like we may never get it. And they're going to leave us anyway.

Our sadness is for ourselves as well as for our parents. We're startled to think that we're soon to become the senior members of the family. As we face our parents' mortality, we also come face-to-face with our own. Tom said, "This is scary stuff. Now I'm going to be the patriarch, but I don't want that. I'm a doer, not a rule giver." We may not be aware of it yet, but we're beginning to grieve.

What we are aware of is this: Our parents need help. Most adult children want to do the "right" thing, to take care of our parents no matter how difficult and uncooperative they might be. We want to make sure their living conditions are clean. We want them to have decent nutrition and the proper medications. We want them to be safe, both at home and out in the world.

For most of us, caregiving means going home again. We may not be physically in our childhood home, but our hearts and minds are about to return to our past. We're returning to help our aging parents because our conscience won't let us walk away, because this is another opportunity to break any cycle of dysfunction in our family, and because this is our last chance to make peace with them while they're alive.

Some of us, however, may need to pause before agreeing to care for our parents. Our anger and resentment toward them may be so strong that the smallest stressor—and there are many in eldercare—could cause us to lose self-control and lash out verbally or physically at them. If our parents harmed us years ago, we may be at risk to harm them now.

Any behavior that makes elders feel vulnerable—yelling at them, mismanaging their finances, slapping and hitting them, depriving them of food and water, ignoring their pleas for help—is considered elder abuse. If we feel we are capable of mistreating our parents, or any other family member for that matter, we need to get help immediately. It's time to call in relatives or friends or senior services agencies to help our parents. It's time for us to get therapy and start dealing with our propensity for anger and violence. Otherwise, we'll be perpetuating the family cycle of abuse.

# THREE

## LOSING INDEPENDENCE

In a perfect world, our parents would remain happily independent, and when they need help, they would ask for it. In reality, it's more likely that our parents will insist they are "doing fine," regardless of the evidence. They'll drive when they can't see. They'll eat a box of crackers rather than prepare a meal. They'll stop bathing altogether when it's too hard to step in and out of the bathtub. They'll let trash and newspapers accumulate in the house when it's too cold, too hot, too heavy, too hard to take the garbage to the curb.

At times, our parents' behavior may not be what it appears to be, and in the same way we deal with young children, we sometimes have to become interpreters for our parents. We need to translate talk and behavior and look for signs in order to figure out what's really going on. Instead of saying, "Mom's irritable today," we need to ask ourselves why she's so irritable. Is she hot? Hungry? Thirsty? Does she need more rest? Is she calling all the time because she's bored or is she afraid?

Keeping tabs on how the parents are doing and determining whether they need some assistance become the caregiver's tasks, but it may be hard for us to assess the situation objectively. While our goal matches our parents' goal—to keep them as independent as possible for as long as possible—the point of contention will be in how we define that objective.

To the caregivers, *getting help* for our parents means Mom and Dad can remain independent. To many parents, however, *accepting help* signals the end of their self-reliance. We say "assistance," but they hear "no longer capable."

Some parents clearly need assistance, but they dig in, resisting change, refusing help, determined to prove that they're still independent. "We're fine." "We've always done it this way." They refuse to accept help without first putting up a big fight. We find ourselves struggling against a closed family system.

Others seem too needy, all too happy to hand over responsibility for their lives to their adult children. They phone us to do this or bring them that or take them somewhere else—and all the requests are for things that our parents are still capable of doing themselves. Richard said, "My dad abandoned us years ago, and now he wants me to find him a job and a place to live."

Christine said, "When my mother told me it was 'up to me,' all I could think was how it had always been up to me."

## COMMUNICATION

When it is obvious that our parents need help with many of the activities of daily living, discussing these issues can be very sensitive, especially if good communication skills between family members have never been established. Certainly, it is easier to have this discussion if we are talking about future needs rather than present problems. Although caregivers are inclined to take action immediately, it is better if we can limit ourselves to offering recommendations and let our parents make the decision. It takes patience, but it's one way to respect and support our parents' desire for independence.

Some parents may say, "We'll deal with it when the time comes."

The difficulty comes when their adult children are compelled to reply, "But Mom and Dad, that time is now."

As much as possible, caregivers need to learn to stay a few steps ahead of their parents' decline. We need to do our homework, educating ourselves about their ongoing aches and pains, their illnesses, their chronic conditions, getting ready for what might happen next. Does today's bum knee mean surgery next year? Are Mom's allergies going to cause any respiratory problems later on?

When we talk to them, we should try to make it as comfortable as possible for them and us. We can present our concerns, ideas, and reasons quietly and gently. We can encourage them to express their feelings, listening carefully to their ideas, trying to understand and acknowledge their fears. We can ask one question at a time, taking care to allow our parents time to think and speak.

These conversations can be difficult because of our feelings. We are educating ourselves about something our parents may have refused to acknowledge. Perhaps they continued to abuse their bodies with cigarettes and alcohol long after they were made aware of the consequences. Or perhaps our parents paid little attention to us when we were young, yet expect us to step up to the plate for them now. We feel resentful and guilty and confused all at once. We're beginning to get a glimpse of what lies ahead.

It will be helpful if we're prepared to have these talks over a period of several days or weeks. Although our parents might balk at some of our early suggestions, given time to think it over, they may have a change of heart. After a few days or weeks, they might be more amenable to our suggestions, especially if convinced they thought of the ideas themselves.

### DRIVING

Driving is often a thorny issue for adult children as they watch their parents become a hazard to themselves and others on the road. "It's the teenage years in reverse," said Doug.

Yet to our parents, a driver's license is proof positive that they are capable, independent, vital. "What if there's an emergency? I might need to rush someone to the hospital," Louise's father said, ignoring the fact that having had two heart attacks already, any emergency was likely to feature him.

Asking our parents to stop driving is easier said than done. It's hard for us to bring up the subject, and it's hard for our parents to hear it. If our families have never solved problems well, it won't happen easily now.

We can appeal to their values, reminding them of what they hold dear—the necessity for safe travel, the rights of pedestrians, obligations to keep passengers safe. We can advise them of the terrible consequences of an accident, where lives as well as property might be lost.

Gloria was ready to take away her mother's car. Because of her mother's dementia, Gloria decided to appeal to her maternal instincts. "We're worried about your driving," said Gloria gently. "We're afraid you might harm a child."

Although not often rational, Gloria's mother responded with great sanity. "I would never want to do that," she said and handed over her car keys.

Not all parents respond to our appeals. Sometimes we have to be ready to jump when the opportunity presents itself. Mike's father was cantankerous, difficult, and couldn't see well. However, one afternoon he was so frightened by a near miss that he called Mike, saying he had no business driving anymore. Mike and his wife rushed to his father's house to take away the car before Dad changed his mind. Sure enough, Dad was furious the next day, but the deed was done. Mike was relieved, even if his father was not.

Some adult children work with their local department of motor vehicles. They encourage their parents to sign up for seniors-only driving classes. When a senior passes the course, the adult child can feel assured that it's okay for the parent to drive.

Many states now require seniors to pass a driving skills test every year or two in order to renew their licenses. Kent's father could not complete a three-point turn, a required skill in North Carolina. Kent sympathized with his father but was secretly grateful to know his dad was no longer behind the wheel of a car.

Yet no matter how gently we state our reasons, our parents might not accept them. When parents refuse to see that they have become a clear danger to themselves and others, there is sometimes no choice but to disable the car or take away the keys.

The issue is only made worse when the adult children fall back on dysfunctional tactics to solve problems. For example, we may decide to lie, offering excuses like "the mechanic said your car can't be fixed." When parents sense that they're being hoodwinked, their hostility and mistrust escalate. They may make phone calls to the garage, or to whomever they think is thwarting their driving. Martin's father made repeated calls to the doctor's office, demanding a letter saying he was fit to drive.

In the end, it's usually better to tell the truth and do what has to be done. There will still be hostility and mistrust, but at least everything is out in the open and others don't have to participate in our lies.

The driving issue is complicated because once we get our parents away from the wheel, other problems arise. How will they get groceries? What about trips to the doctor or pharmacy? Who will chauffeur them around?

For those seniors who live in a large metropolitan area, city transportation—buses, taxis, and subways—is available. They may no longer feel safe in the city, however, or they can't walk very far or they lose their way too easily or they're lugging an oxygen tank around.

For those who live in rural or suburban areas, automobiles are the primary, and perhaps only, means of transportation. Although biking and walking are possible, these may not be practical. Once the parent no longer drives, the transportation burden falls on the caregiver. Now grocery shopping, medical appointments, social occasions, trips to the beauty salon, and more have to be scheduled well in advance and coordinated with other plans.

## NUTRITION

Nutrition—or lack of it—can be a major problem for seniors. It typically becomes an issue when the family chef is no longer able to or interested in preparing regular meals. The effect is compounded with restricted diets, daily medications, and a dollop of stubbornness. Changes in eating habits can be gradual, so caregivers might be unaware for a long period of time that poor nutrition is a problem.

In many families, one parent does most of the cooking. But if that parent is erratic in preparing meals or even stops cooking altogether, the spouse's health will suffer too. Daily meal delivery can be a good solution. Agencies like Meals on Wheels deliver meals to seniors for a nominal fee. Meals are prepared with senior nutritional needs in mind. Meals at restaurants or friends' homes then become extras rather than the mainstay.

Martha's father had never prepared a meal. Widowed at eighty-two, he was not about to learn, so Martha made arrangements for Meals on Wheels to deliver daily.

Medications are another consideration. Check with the doctor or pharmacist to see whether prescribed drugs should be taken with meals or on an empty stomach. There may be temporary restrictions, such as *no alcohol* or *avoid milk products*.

Maureen's mother was continually nauseated from medication after returning home from the hospital because she wasn't eating enough. She understood that her medications needed to be taken with meals but thought one bite of a sandwich would do.

Many seniors are on restricted diets, such as low-sodium to control blood pressure or low-sugar because of diabetes. But if one or both parents no longer have the interest or ability to develop new menus, their health may be jeopardized.

Harry's parents went out for pizza or Chinese food every evening, even though his dad was supposed to be on a low-sodium diet. It was hard to convince Dad that his blood pressure could be more easily controlled simply by finding other restaurants in town.

## PERSONAL HYGIENE

Personal hygiene can be a problem for seniors. Their sense of smell diminishes, their bladders leak, their skin gets drier and tears more easily, they forget that their last bath was several days ago. Caregivers should be on the lookout for changes in personal grooming habits, because such changes can also be symptoms of other problems.

Alice's mother always had taken great pride in her personal appearance, so when she began to watch TV continually and to lounge around in her bathrobe several days a week, Alice knew something was wrong. After an extensive medical evaluation, her mother's depression was diagnosed. After several weeks on a mild antidepressant, she began to take better care of herself. Soon she was up and around, nattily dressed, going out with her friends.

As Amy's mother's dementia increased, she began to store her clothes in the tub, making baths impossible. She also rejected soap, no longer understanding what it was used for. To keep her clean, Amy squirted liquid soap and shampoo on her mother as she got into the shower, knowing she would stay there until she had rinsed the offending liquid off her body.

As we age, we lose muscle strength. The simple act of stepping in and out of a bathtub gets more and more difficult. Seniors who live alone worry they will slip and fall in the shower and that no one will know to rescue them. We can install grab bars in the tub, in the shower, and near the toilet so our parents have a handhold when raising or lowering themselves. We can make sure they have a bath mat or nonskid strips for the bottom of the bathtub or shower stall. Extra security features like these will make cleanliness routines safer and easier.

A musty urine smell caused by a leaky bladder used to be one of the hallmarks of an aging senior. But that no longer needs to be the case. There are protective covers and pads for mattresses and chairs. Today nearly every grocery store carries several brands of special underwear for seniors. These disposable undergarments are specially designed to absorb moisture and neutralize odors. They also help keep the skin dry, minimizing rashes and other skin disorders.

## HOUSEKEEPING

Housekeeping chores take more time and energy as we age, and they can be overwhelming to seniors who are sick or incapacitated. The decisions our parents make about these responsibilities can be a key to their overall physical and mental health.

Because seniors' abilities tend to diminish slowly, caregivers often find that they start doing one small chore for their parents, then another and another, until soon they are overwhelmed with the burden of managing their parents' household. Equally distressing is that adult children are spending their caregiving time on chores rather than talking, listening, and observing. When the chores are done, it's time to leave. The caregiver is tired and cranky—and has to face the same chores again at home—and the senior is disappointed that no real communication took place. Both are upset and dissatisfied because they had no quality time together.

We can deal with some of the housekeeping chores by hiring help. Waste management companies can be hired for weekly pickups of garbage and recycling. A housecleaning service every week or two will keep the house neat, dusted, and vacuumed. Most services will change bed linens and do weekly laundry as well, although an additional fee might be involved. If there are outside yard chores to do, we can hire a lawn service or neighborhood teenager to mow grass during the summer and rake leaves in the fall.

When our parents begin hiring help, they may also begin to worry about their finances. They fret about not being able to afford these services, and in many cases, this may be true.

If finances are an issue, now is the time to examine them closely. Their expenses are likely to increase, requiring them to withdraw from their savings. They may need not only housekeeping services but also additional medications on a regular basis.

The inability to keep up with household chores or afford outside help is likely to trigger a discussion of alternate housing arrangements, including every option from maintenance-free condominiums to nursing homes to living with us. Susan said, "My mother's bedroom is on the second floor of her condo. She can barely manage the stairs now, and I'm worried how much longer she's going to be able to live there on her own."

Although the decision might be to stay put for now, the handwriting is on the wall. Sooner or later, our parents will need to modify their current living arrangements. It's easier to think about various options now rather than wait for a crisis to force the issue.

### MEDICATIONS

Many seniors take a number of daily medications: perhaps a diuretic to help a weak heart, a blood thinner to ward off another stroke, a stool softener to keep the intestines functioning, something for arthritis, and so on down a long list. The older they get, the more likely it is that our parents are being treated by more than one doctor, each specializing in a particular disorder. If one doctor is not told what another is prescribing, the stage is set for drug interactions, being over-medicated, and problems with compliance or addiction.

Edna said, "My mother had a bad heart, glaucoma, and debilitating arthritis. She was seeing a different doctor for each of these problems and getting prescriptions from all of them.

She seemed too lethargic to me, so I made a list of all her drugs and called each doctor. Sure enough, a couple of drugs were changed or stopped, and Mom began to perk up."

Overmedication occurs when an aging body takes longer than average to purge itself of the drug, causing the drug to build up and accumulate in the body over time. Although individual drugs may have been prescribed to treat different symptoms, the effects can overlap. To prevent this, we can keep an updated record of our parents' medications and give it to every doctor who is treating them.

For some seniors, compliance, or the ability to follow directions, can be a problem when taking medications. Where there is a history of addiction, seniors may not want to take the drug as prescribed.

Dean said, "My father's attitude about pills was that if one was good, three were better."

Where one person is inclined to take too much medication, another might not be willing to take any at all. Sharon's mother needed daily medication for her respiratory problems, but she periodically refused, saying, "I'm just not a person who takes a lot of pills."

Compliance can also be an issue if additional directions must be followed. For example, some drugs should be taken with food, others on an empty stomach. Some drugs can be taken during waking hours; others should be taken around the clock. Thus, if the instructions are to take a pill *four times a day,* it's important to find out whether that means *at meals and bedtime* or *every six hours.* If the instructions are to *remain upright for thirty minutes after taking drug,* the caregiver and the senior both need to understand why.

We may need to educate our parents—and ourselves—about any side effects, particularly those that can affect our parent's daily routine. For example, an exercise program may need to be modified if our parent is taking a medication that interferes with the body's natural cooling mechanism or causes dehydration. We can ask the pharmacist or look up each drug in a pharmaceutical dictionary.

Medications can do much to help our parents, easing certain behavior problems as well as reducing pain and making them more comfortable. There are drugs to stimulate their appetite, help them sleep, and reduce cravings for nicotine and alcohol, among other things. Although there is no known preventative medication for Alzheimer's at this time, some drugs can help slow the progress of dementia, helping patients maintain their current mental status for a longer period.

We should also be aware of the possibility that a given medication can have the opposite effect of what was intended. Sometimes an anti-anxiety drug might make our parents more agitated, more belligerent, or more disinhibited. Caregivers should report any physical or behavioral changes that appear to contradict our expectations.

The more seniors and their caretakers know about the drugs being prescribed, the more they can maximize the positive effects. Even if a sure cure isn't possible, knowledge keeps everyone's expectations in line with reality.

## CARING FOR CHILDREN VERSUS CARING FOR PARENTS

By the time our parents need our help, many of us have also been working hard to raise our own children. Because we started with the deficit of not having good models to follow, we learned parenting skills and gained insights by trial and error. We know how to deal with most childhood illnesses— a day or two of rest plus the occasional bottle of medicine seems to cure everything. Sure enough, in short order our little darlings are bounding out of bed, full of energy, ready to take on the world again.

What we soon discover when caring for our parents is that the rules have changed. Our children are growing, getting stronger, healthier, and more independent every year, but the opposite is happening with our parents. They're slowing down and becoming progressively weaker and more dependent.

Caring for children is about celebration and growth. We applaud their first words, first steps, first tooth, new and exciting accomplishments one after another. We take great joy in watching them grow strong and independent. Today they're tying their shoelaces; tomorrow they're driving the car. We urge our children into the future, celebrating the day they get dressed by themselves, the day they learn to ride a bike, the day they get their driver's license, and the day they move into their own apartment.

Caring for our parents is about grief and loss. We watch them grow physically weaker, struggling to manage everyday tasks and becoming increasingly dependent on us. Minor ailments turn into major illnesses—a summer cold turns into pneumonia, a slip on the stairs results in a fractured bone. Each new problem signals another bit of lost independence and another reminder of their continuing decline. We watch our parents face the passing of old skills, old friends, old victories. We start living moment to moment with them, struggling with our own conflicting feelings, trying to be grateful for whatever abilities they still have today, hoping they can continue to manage tomorrow.

# FOUR

## ESTATE ISSUES

One of the early problems that many caregivers have to face has to do with their parents' estates. Doctors want to know whether there is health insurance, hospitals will ask whether our parents have prepared any advance directives regarding medical care, our parents may be too sick this year to file their income tax return. The list of legal and financial issues is long, and there is still the lifetime's worth of stuff that our parents have accumulated.

There is also the problem of not enough or no financial reserves. Agencies can provide financial assistance, but we need to start investigating whether or not our parents are eligible right away. The application process can be lengthy, and government gears often move slowly.

At the same time, we may need to make some decisions regarding how much financial support we can—or are willing to—offer. We may not want to donate our own hard-earned savings for our parents' care, particularly if we feel they never provided for us. Or we may decide we can afford some help, but that means choices for our parents will be limited by our budget. We may feel that a richer relative should assume the financial burden. The issue is not what we choose to do but simply that we make a decision we can live with—a decision that is most appropriate for us.

## ESTATE PLANNING

For some parents, estate planning is another aspect of losing their independence. They resist the idea that they should make plans to hand down what they may have hoarded or guarded all their lives. They equate estate planning with dying. If they're not ready to face their own mortality, they're not going to be interested in preparing a will.

Maria said, "My dad figures the minute he writes a will, he's going to die. I can't get him to talk about it."

When our parents do estate planning, it is more than making their wishes known. Estate planning also means making decisions for themselves, decisions that can tear a family apart when adult children have to decide on their parents' behalf.

Thoughtful planning protects our parents' resources while they are alive, ensuring that their assets can only be used to benefit them and making it difficult for predators, both in and outside the immediate family, to take advantage of them in their old age. Good planning also protects them in the event of dementia, a situation where our parents could very well be their own worst enemies.

Estate planning covers more than what to do about money and property. It also includes instructions regarding what to do if they become mentally or physically incapacitated as well as instructions for their medical care—what our parents want done under certain circumstances, and who should be in charge. We may not agree with what our parents choose, but the decisions are theirs, not ours. As long as their wishes are crystal clear, there can be little argument among the adult children later on.

Caregivers often have to confront these issues right away, typically regarding healthcare for their parents. Doctors and hospitals want to know about health insurance, living wills, who is authorized to make healthcare decisions if the parents are unable to act on their own, and more. In some cases, caregivers may not be able to get medical help for their parents, other than life-or-death emergency care, until they have this information in hand.

Convincing a stubborn parent takes time and patience. We can only respond to what they say. We can be firm without being adamant. Our parents can be like young children at times, so we have to act accordingly. We introduce the idea, knowing there will be resistance. Over the next few months, we bring it up a few more times, hoping to persuade them with kind and gentle persistence until they get used to the idea.

The truth is, adult children have to get used to the idea too. None of us wants to think that the time has come for us to be involved in our parents' affairs. We'd rather assume that what they say is correct. If they get inflexible when we press them, it's easier to back off.

Some parents are sure the planning they did thirty years ago is still fine. Chances are, it is not. Inheritance laws are amended from time to time, both at the state and federal level. These laws also vary from state to state, so what is valid in one state might not be accepted in another. One way to get things moving is to have a professional, someone outside the family, do the talking. Even then, our parents may not admit what they finally heard, but their behaviors may indicate otherwise.

Jackie was worried that her father's will was not in accordance with current estate and tax laws: "He had just moved to another state, and besides that, his original attorney was an alcoholic. So my sister and I badgered him, finally offering to pay the fees if his new attorney told him everything was in order. Next thing we knew, he was setting up trusts, signing a new will, and so forth, but he never acknowledged we were right. We didn't care; we were happy to see that he was finally getting his affairs in order."

We need to remember that our families change over time. They are extended and blended with marriages, deaths, divorces, minor children, adult children, in-laws, ex-laws, and outlaws. "My brother died without a will, about a year after my dad passed away," said Joseph. "It got complicated because my dad's estate hadn't been settled yet, we all lived in different states, and none of the lawyers were sure what to do with my brother's share."

Finally, we need to know where our parents keep their important papers. Insurance policies, wills, stocks and bonds, property deeds, and the like are useless if we can't find them. Is there a safe-deposit box? Is an attorney holding these papers? Should we be looking under the mattress?

If our parents are reluctant to share this information, we can provide a notebook with blanks for them to fill in, promising to look only if they are incapacitated. Or we can suggest that they give the notebook to another trusted family member, or to an outside authority figure such as a banker or lawyer. It's worth it to keep pestering them until we're confident the information is available to somebody somewhere.

### FAMILY HEIRLOOMS

Family heirlooms are reminders of our past—that other generations have gone before us, that we're part of a family chain. When these keepsakes are passed from one generation to another, they become links that join the generations, touchstones for a family's oral history. When our elders pass

them on to us, we are honored to be chosen as this generation's guardian of the family keepsake. It's as if our branch of
the family tree is now given official status.

Donna said, "My grandfather was a farmer, and one day
while plowing his field, he found two arrowheads. He never
found any more, just those two. He passed them on to my
mother, and now my sister and I each have one."

On the other hand, family keepsakes can be major issues
among adult children. The point is not necessarily the dollar
value of the item—an inexpensive watch might be as treas-
ured as a large sapphire ring. The issue is what that item sym-
bolizes, or the emotional value that family members have
vested in it. When a family is dysfunctional, when emotional
needs weren't met, keepsakes can become substitutes for affection. We feel that we didn't get enough love and attention,
so we're "owed" the family heirloom or we "deserve" any
extra cash left in the family coffers.

Michelle described her mother's funeral. "While the rest
of us were having breakfast, my brother went to the bank and
emptied out her account. What surprised me was that he
didn't need the money, and there wasn't much there anyway.
He also had the funeral director remove my mother's jewelry
and give it to him. My sister, who was very wealthy, decided
that she was going to keep all the money from the life insurance policy. Again, we're not talking much money here, and
Mother had always said it was for her funeral expenses. So
my husband and I paid for the funeral, and I never spoke to
either of them [brother and sister] again."

Lisa's mother refused to say who was to inherit Grandmother's ring. Lisa said, "My sister told my brother that Mom
had promised her the ring. She [sister] wouldn't say that to
me because we both know that's not true. I've asked Mom
several times to update her will or at least make a list saying

who gets what, but she hasn't done it and isn't about to. If Mom wants her to have it, that's fine with me. What bothers me is that my sister is laying claim to it behind Mom's back."

Most professionals urge seniors to distribute their assets in a way that will keep the family together afterward. However, this may not happen. Parents may prefer one child over another, or siblings don't trust each other, or members of an extended family have never been able to get along.

Angela said, "Mama, decide now where you want your treasures to go. I will not challenge my stepbrother and sister. Whatever you want to distribute, do it now while you're living. Once you're gone, nothing equitable will happen."

We need to remember that "fair" and "equal" are not necessarily the same thing. If one adult child has been running the family business, it is probably fair for that person to inherit the business, even though doing so would mean the estate is not distributed equally, dollar for dollar. On the other hand, even though one adult child has assumed most of the caregiving burden in the parents' last years, it might be unfair to give that sibling a larger share than the others.

Where there are considerable funds, some adult children get itchy to get their hands on "their" financial inheritance before their parents have died. Common rationales include "I need it now, so why should I wait." Or "Better me than a nursing home." Or "Better me than the IRS." Or "After what they put me through, they owe me." Or "After all the grief she gave me, I deserve it."

Adult children don't necessarily know the financial status of their parents. What we assume to be true might not be so. Lynne said, "I always thought my folks had plenty of money, but when my dad died, we discovered that there was almost nothing. We had to scramble to sell the house and get something set up for my mother."

We need to remember that any money or property our parents have is their money, not ours. We did not earn it, and we may not necessarily inherit it. In fact, most people need, and spend, their entire savings during the last few years of their lives for medical, pharmaceutical, and living expenses.

## LETTING GO

Many caregiving issues have to do with letting go, and one of the first places we can practice letting go involves the choices our parents make. We have to let go of the fact that our parents, who may have made bad choices in the past, may still be making unwise choices about their health, their finances, and their housing, among other things. They may also make poor choices regarding who is trustworthy and who is not. We can offer suggestions, get professional advice, but in the end, how our parents handle their affairs is up to them. We may have to work hard against stepping into old family dialogues and dynamics, but we can learn to let go.

Gary said, "When my mother died, there was a trust fund that my father managed. Unfortunately he couldn't wrap his mind around the tax issues, so he made decisions that cost him a great deal of money. There was no convincing him; he wouldn't listen to his accountant, much less me."

Anne said, "My stepfather let his daughter have control of his finances, which was a big mistake because she spent much of his money on herself. It's very sad because if he had been willing to take his attorney's advice, his savings could have been managed safely and conservatively, and there would have been sufficient funds to see him through his last years."

Lynda said, "My mother is in a nursing home, and the squabbling over who gets what has already started. It's too bad she wouldn't make any decisions about her money and car and jewelry while she was able."

It is especially hard to let go when our emotional needs weren't fully met when we were children. We're adults, but the family treasure has become an important symbol. We didn't get enough love, so the Indian Head pennies or Dad's fishing lures or Mom's jewelry will have to do. And we're willing to fight for it. We want it, we need it, we've earned it, we deserve it.

Sue said, "My brother pockets stuff every time he visits the folks. He's always nosing around in the boxes in the basement."

Tom said, "I suggested to my brother that we put Mom's jewelry in a safe-deposit box, and he got huffy. 'Why would I know where Mom put it?' Sure enough, I checked Mom's jewelry box and her emerald ring was already gone."

Every adult child has his or her own perspective regarding Mom's and Dad's estate. What makes sense to one may seem unforgivable to another. We can't control how others think and act, however. Nothing we do or say will change their minds. The only thing we can do is let go of their behavior and pay closer attention to our own.

Perhaps deep in our caregiving hearts, we secretly think all this help of ours will be rewarded. We tell ourselves that we're going to do the extra caregiving so we can be sure and get our share. Perhaps our parents have even promised us a deferred reward, saying, "After I'm gone, I want you to have the _____." But much of the time we don't get that reward, at least not in the way we think we will.

Bobbi said, "About a month before she died, my mother told me I could have this old clock. When I told my brother later, he said, 'I knew it! You took advantage of Mom! She wanted *me* to have the clock!' And he grabbed it off the shelf and walked out of the house."

Our parents' belongings can be a real tyranny. We have to ask ourselves whether one crystal bowl is going to replace the years of loving that we didn't get when we really needed it. If we're trying to compensate for something we didn't get in our childhood, caregiving won't do it. Mom's cookbook collection and Dad's boat won't do it either.

Letting go of our parents' possessions makes us free. We're free when we know in our hearts that their stuff no longer matters. We grew up without it, we have created a life for ourselves without it, we have the love of friends and spouse and children. We don't need those treasures now. Even though we're the caregivers, we can make peace with what we didn't get in our childhood.

This can be one of our first moments of freedom: accepting that we're not going to get the treasure we'd like to have, accepting that somebody else is going to take it, accepting that our parents may not give us our fair share. If our parents refuse to get their affairs in order, unfortunately there's not much we can do except this: We can let go.

We're free when we can remind ourselves that we're not owed an inheritance. Our parents' estate belongs to them, not us. They are entitled to do with it whatever they want, including rolling down the car window and throwing their money in the street.

We're free when we cleanse our spirit of the need for those possessions, when we decide to nurture ourselves in other ways. We're free when we recognize that the "stuff" is simply a symbol, compensation, a way of hanging on to the past.

# 11

# I Can't Cope!

## Reengaging the Past

# FIVE

## FAMILY ISSUES

Caregiving takes us back to our roots, back to the family we were raised in, back to the system that gave us our first notion of what the world is like and how it works. Our family of origin was our first universe, and it's to this world that we're returning as caregivers. We may have changed, but the family system is probably about like it was when we left.

We may very well have a good intellectual handle on our family of origin. Perhaps we've sought counseling in an effort to come to terms with unresolved issues from our past. We understand what happened, and we've gone on with our lives. We've worked hard to become separate individuals in our own right. But this understanding will be put to the test when we become caregivers to our parents. We are testing our knowledge in an entirely new life event, but on an old battleground with well-known companions.

By looking at the family as a whole, we can begin to see how it affects our views on aging and whether the family system will help or hinder our caregiving efforts. Today we have psychological insights that were not available to our parents. We can be more perceptive about our families, for we have the tools, if we choose to use them, to untangle some of the family myths and dysfunctions.

If we try once again to deal with old family issues before we lose our parents, we'll be doing ourselves a great favor. Once they're gone, it's too late to make up, too late to apologize, too late to ask for their version of past events, too late to ask about their feelings. It will be too late to tell them whatever it is we need to say.

If we sort things out now, we can change the way we respond to our parents. If we can learn to react appropriately to current situations, we won't be left with guilty feelings about our harsh words and insensitive actions. It's easy to be frustrated with our parents when they're alive and making us crazy with their demands, their dementia, their needs. But after they're gone, is that what we want to be left with? Our aggravation and resentment? Our guilt about what we said? Our remorse over what we didn't say?

Brian said, "I was reading figures to my dad and he was posting them in the ledger. I was upset with him because he made so many mistakes—reversing numbers, entering them on the wrong line, that kind of thing. I was pretty hard on him, and I feel terrible about it now. I wish I had realized how sick he was."

If we're going to take care of our parents, we're going to have to face some old family issues. We're going to reengage our past to get a better understanding of today's caregiving problems because many of these issues are rooted in the past. But if we work through these issues, we'll be free to be present for our parents *wherever they're at today*. We don't have to be drawn back into the behavior patterns of our youth. We can learn healthier, more appropriate ways to respond to our parents. This is an opportunity for us. It's a chance to make a difference in ourselves, in our feelings about our parents, and in our relationship with them.

## WHAT KIND OF FAMILY
## DID I GROW UP IN?

Every family is faced with challenges and crises from time to time—injuries, illness, moving to a new town, accepting a new job, losing an old job, a child with special needs, marital problems, financial woes, and more. These are typical of the difficult life events that confront us all sooner or later. It's not the event itself that we need to look at, but instead how our family deals with life's ups and downs. What is normal and what is not? What is a healthy reaction and what is a dysfunctional response?

In a functional family, the interactions, behaviors, and relationships work to benefit the family as a whole. Each family member has a job. The children's job is to play and explore; the parents' job is to care for their children. No one person is rewarded consistently at the expense of another. Healthy parents protect their children as best they can, nourishing them in body and spirit, helping them to develop and grow. For example, Bill made sure he was there to cheer for any school sport in which one of his sons was playing. He spent countless hours watching his boys play soccer, hockey, and baseball.

Healthy families understand that difficult times are part of life and happen to everyone. When disaster strikes, the family may be surprised, but members also assume they can figure out a way around and through the problems, coming closer together in the process. They know any event can be exasperating, complicated, formidable, even traumatic, but they assume it is doable. They expect to persevere. At the same time, family members are quick to recognize new or abnormal behavior in each other.

In a dysfunctional family, the interactions, behaviors, and relationships do not work to benefit the family as a whole.

People aren't doing their jobs—parents behave like kids, children are thrust into adult roles, addiction or mental illness dictates behavior, a parent abandons the family, adults are abusing each other, children are ignored and unprotected.

An all too common situation is when one parent has a serious drinking problem and the other family members are involved in a constant cover-up and denial. "Mom is sleeping and can't come to the phone right now," might be a familiar refrain. In this case, Mom's drinking has involved other family members; it is an ongoing family crisis.

Dysfunctional families fall apart easily. Every difficult situation becomes a catastrophe. Every problem is indeed a disaster. When problems arise, family members feel overwhelmed, thinking, *The problem is bigger than I am. I can't survive this.* In addition, because dysfunction is the norm within the family, there is already a high tolerance for abnormal behavior. Thus, actions or responses that signal a need for help are likely to be overlooked.

Caregivers often fall into the trap of trying to fix the family dysfunction. We think that if John does this and Mary does that, then our parents will do something else and all will be well. Yet John and Mary and our parents don't—or won't—do what we suggest, and nothing gets fixed, nothing changes, and we just don't understand why no one listens to us.

What we need to understand is this: whatever the family has been, that's the way it's going to stay. There may be fancier explanations now, more elaborate excuses, but the main family structure, dysfunctional or not, is going to be just as it always was.

## FAMILY MYTHS, FAMILY SCRIPTS

Every family has its own set of scripts and rules, many of which can be healthy and beneficial. "We value higher education and advanced training." "We are physically fit." "We participate in team sports." "We are business entrepreneurs." "We are not afraid of hard work." "We take care of ourselves and others." "We enjoy music and dance." "If you want it enough, you can make it happen."

These myths and scripts become rooted in our family traditions and the stories we pass along—the picnic when the rowboat sank, the time the dog chased Uncle Tony up the drainpipe, how great-great-grandfather Reginald was a Buffalo Soldier, how Aunt Sally's daughters and granddaughters are nurses, and look how we always posed for pictures by the big elm tree in front of Grandma's house. If we define ourselves by these myths and scripts, and if the scripts are useful, they can serve us well. They help us think and act in a positive light, perhaps as a public servant or hard worker or simply someone who reads a lot.

Other myths and scripts are not so healthy. "It's someone else's fault." "People don't like us." "Sick people are lazy." "We're entitled to special treatment." "Rules are for other people, not us." "Playing is a waste of time." "We take care of our own." "Our relatives are an embarrassment." "We don't tell other people our business."

Sometimes these labels are put on the children, whether true or not, whether kind or not. We are labeled as smart, dumb, helpful, rebellious, pretty, homely, athletic, sickly, and so on. We change, but the label may stick. We hang on to these definitions whether they're useful or not.

We also learn to deal with caregiving according to the family script. We do what was modeled for us. Our expectations are based on what we learned early on. Sally said, "My mother took care of my grandmother, and I'm taking care of Mom. When the time comes, my daughters will take care of me."

We tend to be loyal to these scripts and myths, even when they're inappropriate. Ellen said, "Basically I did what my parents wanted me to do. It took a therapist to help me see that I had some choices and that it would be okay to do things differently. Finally I did make some changes, but boy, did the family resent it. It was hard for me to get over the fact that they were never going to understand and certainly weren't going to approve. From their point of view, I was being disloyal."

"That's the way we do it in this family" doesn't make it an ultimate truth. It's simply the way our family did it. We forget—or maybe we didn't know—that there are many ways to handle a situation. A dysfunctional family script doesn't allow for the fact that there are other choices. It's the family way, period. We may need to understand that it's okay to consider other choices. Some choices are better, some worse, some about the same, but there are always choices.

What we need to be aware of is that old messages from our childhood, inappropriate family scripts that have been with us our entire life, can interfere with our role as caregiver. If we felt that we did not measure up as a child— if we were not good enough, athletic enough, tall enough, smart enough—we are probably going to feel inadequate as caregivers.

We may be unaware that we, as caregivers, are really carrying two burdens. We carry not only the effects of inappropriate messages from a closed, rigid family, messages we learned when we were younger, but we also bear the weight of the caregiving situation today. Much of the time, we are working on problems from both the present and the past.

Virginia said, "My mother used to tell me I was not a good Christian, so any time I decide to be with my husband and kids instead of doing for her, I feel guilty and wonder whether I'm being selfish."

Jack said, "I'm paying all my mother's bills and supporting

her in the nursing home, and she still tells me I'll never amount to anything."

Even if we were once slapdash and lackadaisical in our approach to life, that is no longer true, for the situation has changed. We are switching places with our parents, caring for them, becoming their guardians. We are mature now, with adult responsibilities. And no matter what we were told years ago, today we can choose to be competent and capable.

## FAMILY ROLES

Within each family, members often assume—or are assigned—certain roles. Some roles are healthy, some not. When the roles of the children in the family are dysfunctional, the effects stay with them well into their adult lives. Thus, when children are asked to solve adult problems, they become adult codependents, fine-tuned to recognize other people's needs at the expense of their own.

Nicole was the problem solver among her siblings. Her mother had been injured and needed daily help until she was back on her feet. The four adult children had a family conference to decide how to handle the situation. Nicole described what happened. "The youngest one just walked out of the room, and no one said, 'Come back.' Then the other two turned to me. They had their excuses about their jobs, couldn't afford time off, whatever. But since I was a stay-at-home mom, they felt I was free to stay and care for our mother. The worst part is, I went along with them. I left my husband and teenage son and spent eight weeks with Mom. What was I thinking?"

Sibling roles generally don't change. Rather than whine and grouse and argue, we're better off trying to identify what our old roles were and what they mean now that we're adults. The roles we had when growing up are good indicators of how we'll interact with others and how we'll face our caregiving duties. In short, the way family members are interacting now is probably the same way they have always interacted.

Even when we have changed, we're likely to revert to our old roles for a time, especially in a crisis or under prolonged stress. The baby of the family is happy not to assume any of the caregiving duties. The family rebel again threatens to walk away. The quiet one offers no suggestions, but complains about being ignored. The bossy one begins to bark orders. The controlling one takes over. Sooner or later, we need to face the reality that what we see from the rest of our family is exactly what we're going to get, over and over again.

### CAREGIVER ROLES

In a family with several adult children, the role of caregiver typically falls on one or two of the adult children, usually (but not necessarily) whoever lives nearest the parents. From a practical point of view, it's easier to have one sibling assume the primary responsibility for monitoring the parents. Problems arise when old roles, old relationships, old issues start to surface.

The adult child most likely to be a primary caregiver is a daughter who lives close to the parents. Adult daughters, especially those who are already wives and mothers, tend to jump to the role of hands-on caregiver. Adult sons, on the other hand, are more likely to see themselves as care managers and are more willing to look for help outside the immediate family.

There are other reasons that we might find ourselves in a

caregiver role. Perhaps we're the one in the family who needs to be in control. Or we're the one most enmeshed with the parent. Or we've always been the problem solver in the family. Or we're the most trustworthy. Or we have the most financial resources. Or we're the one operating from the most fear—fear that another sibling might not be as thorough or as careful, fear that we'll be blamed for our parents' demise. Or no one else will do it.

Most adult children have no recollection of making a conscious choice to be the caregiver. We just evolved into the role. In the beginning, we had no real understanding of what caregiving was all about. We just started doing what needed to be done. Caregiving just sort of happened, and before we knew it, we were in the throes of it.

At some point, the reasons no longer matter. We grow into the reality of being a caregiver. We sometimes wonder how we ended up doing this, yet we never let go of our responsibilities. We grow into the decision we've made, and in the process, we grow in integrity.

## DEALING WITH TODAY

The way Mom and Dad are handling being old reflects the way they handled most things in their lives. Their behavior, their decisions, their ability to be happy are fairly predictable, if we stop and think about how they were earlier in their lives. If they were unreasonable in their younger days, they're likely to be just as bad tempered in their senior years, and even more so.

Claire recalls her parents as avoiding decisions, especially difficult ones. "They were never able to sit down and discuss the pros and cons with one another. They'd just put their heads in the sand and wait until the situation resolved itself one way or another. Then it was never their choice—or their fault."

Sandra describes her father as being controlling. "As he got older and more frail, he got more controlling about the minutiae of his life—was the front door locked, and did I put the garbage on the north side of the driveway, and did I remember to put his washcloth on the left side of the bathroom basin?"

Chris said, "My dad was always demanding, but it got worse as he got older. At the end of his life, he was an emotional bully. He was nasty to all of us who were taking care of him."

Betty said, "My mother seemed to get more passive as she got older. She was sick a lot too, but she never seemed to fight it."

Jeff said, "My dad was very impulsive. I think he made a lot of big decisions when he'd had too many drinks. He'd accept a new job, buy a second house, that kind of stuff, when he'd had a snoot full. It was tough on my mom."

Russell said, "My dad made all the decisions, and my mom liked that. But when he died, she had no idea how to run her life. She'd only run the house. She'd never paid a bill, and she wasn't all that thrilled about learning. She expected us kids to jump right in and pick up where Dad left off."

Lorraine said, "My parents were truly soul mates. In fact, Dad was the love of my mother's life. Everything else was secondary, including their children. They decided everything together. After he died, she continued to pursue Dad's business dream, even though it proved to be a hopeless cause."

Many of us find it hard to say that our parents are dysfunctional, especially in their later years. They're barely able to care for themselves, and we're heavyhearted to see them aging at an alarming rate. We feel disloyal and ungrateful even to suggest that they're making poor decisions and have become more difficult than ever.

The problem is most of us are used to our parents and how they run their lives, so even their dysfunctional patterns are "normal" to us. We can tolerate their poor choices because their way of thinking is so familiar and predictable. Further, to disagree is likely to cause a major family ruckus, so we hesitate to question a long-established, rigid family pattern. It's hard to express our doubts regarding what is happening or ask ourselves whether what we see is unreasonable. It's much easier to believe the situation is okay because it has always been that way.

Harold said, "My mother was in the hospital being detoxed from prescription pain medicine. When I checked her medicine cabinet, sure enough, she had a huge stash of pills. There were all her favorites and most of them were very addictive, but I didn't throw them away because it would have upset her. I wouldn't hesitate now, but back then, I was too caught up in the family system to take issue with it."

Jennifer said, "My father-in-law is eighty-nine and drives himself to dialysis twice a week. I don't see why my friends think it's a bad idea. He just won't have it any other way."

Even if we're hesitant to label our parents as dysfunctional, we might know in our hearts that there are better ways to handle a crisis than was modeled for us. If we're going to keep ourselves from slipping into old roles, we'll have to look for better solutions and learn new ways to respond.

For example, if we are aware of addiction issues, we can talk to our parents, but in many cases they will ignore us or deny the problem. We can make sure their doctors are informed, and we can seek counseling for ourselves, looking for help as we struggle to care for them in spite of their poor choices. When we understand how the family system works, and our part in it, we are getting ready to redefine ourselves and expand our role choices within the family structure.

The point is, our parents won't change, but we can. Our parents and other members of our family may be irrational and unreasonable, but we can keep our cool and act sensibly. We can't control what other family members say or think or do, but we can be in charge of ourselves. They may not believe us, but we can believe in ourselves. They may continue to be abusive, but we can choose to stop being victimized. They may not listen, may not cooperate, but that's okay. We can trust ourselves to care for our parents as best we can.

# SIX

=======================

## COPING ISSUES FOR
## THE ADULT CHILD

Returning to the family fold as a caregiver is highly charged because we're going to the source of our issues. All the old stuff starts to resurface, and it is complicated—and intensified—by the crisis of our parents' decline. Each member of the family is in a different emotional place. Our siblings are adults with families and lives of their own, after all, yet we tend to revert to who we were and how we felt many years ago. The family tries to handle this crisis the same way it addressed struggles in the past.

To be a caregiver is to be on an emotional roller coaster that seems like it will never stop. We go from collapsing in tears to stomping around in anger. We eat ourselves up with guilt because we can't make our parents stronger, healthier, or younger, and at the same time we resent having to try. We're bitter about the care and attention we needed, but didn't get, from our parents. We find ourselves doing for them what they did not do for us.

Jane said, "Mom didn't have compassion for me, but I'm supposed to have compassion for her?"

Charles said, "My dad doesn't remember much about my

childhood because he 'was working and wasn't around much.' But he makes it clear that it's my job to take care of him. It's hard not to resent that."

How we feel colors our relationship with everyone around us, our friends, our spouses, our children, and even ourselves. We struggle with our fears, feeling helpless and depressed. We resent advice even as we pray for help. We get angry and start blaming others. We obsess with our friends and worry ourselves to sleep.

Our emotions can easily become roadblocks in the caregiving and limit our ability to cope effectively. We say yes when we want to say no, we blame ourselves for our parents' problems, or we help too much or too little. If we're going to remove these emotional barriers, we need to take another look at our early years and what our parents modeled for us.

## HOW FAMILIES HANDLE EMOTIONS

Our family of origin is where we learned the language of emotions. Here is where we learned which emotions were acceptable and which were not, and which were to be avoided at all costs. We learned to react to life the way our parents, or our primary caregivers, did.

In a healthy family, many emotions are experienced and then released. As life events occur, the family works through them from beginning to end. The adult child from this kind of family is not afraid of painful feelings like anger or grief. It's okay to laugh; it's okay to cry. Emotions are not to be feared or avoided; our emotions are to be experienced and acknowledged as a normal part of life.

Healthy families also aim their emotions at the right target: the present situation, the current state of affairs. These family members may be annoyed with the extra work and worry but not with their parents per se. They are concerned about their parents' increasing dependency, yet they accept the situation for what it is. They get angry with the sibling who isn't trustworthy, not the driver in the car ahead and not the clerk behind the counter.

In a dysfunctional family, only a few emotions are expressed. Responses become rigid, appearing again and again, whether appropriate to the situation or not.

Claudia said, "My mom always looked for a scapegoat, someone else to blame. When she got fired, it was a co-worker's fault. When she had a stroke, it was my father's fault."

Robert said, "Avoidance was big in my house. Whenever there was a problem, Dad would pour himself a stiff drink, and Mom would take a sleeping pill. No discussion. Problem solved."

When we deny our deepest feelings, they will eventually appear anyway, often as an unexpected binge of rage or tears or depression. We rage at the world when a sigh of annoyance would be enough, or we are wracked with sobs at a movie when everyone else is quietly shedding a tear or two. When our emotions are too intense and out of sync with the situation, then our past is coming into the present.

Not surprisingly, if we are from a dysfunctional family, we probably have a limited set of responses, mostly feeling the one emotion that feels safest for us. We become emotionally rigid, as though stuck in one feeling. Other emotions are bottled up and ignored. When new emotions bubble up, self-doubt surfaces, so we suppress the insecurity, returning again and again to the emotion that is safest, the one we're most comfortable with. We bellow, we cry, we pout, we whine, we find somebody to blame, we get depressed. Our favorite emotion becomes our comfort zone. We use it like a drug to keep our anxiety under control.

Peggy said, "When my life seems out of control, I get upset about the house. I want all the stuff put away, every room clean and tidy, everything impossibly perfect."

Della said, "I hate to admit it, but it's easy for me to get mad. It's *sad* that's scary for me. I'd much rather be yelling than crying."

Some caregivers grew up in homes where alcohol and other drugs were used to quell anxiety, so we may have learned to do that too. Even though we're in recovery from substance abuse now, we will have to be careful not to return to our old addiction or substitute a new one like shopping or smoking or overeating.

### CAREGIVER EMOTIONS

The challenge for caregivers is to make sure that we are responding to the situation, not to our emotions. When we stay in our emotional comfort zone, we limit our responses, and as a result, we limit our ability to cope with the situation. If we feel guilty all the time, we'll act in ways that add to the guilt. If we are easily aroused to anger, we'll lash out at those around us. If we feel helpless, we'll stop in our tracks, unable to cope, waiting for someone—a friend, our spouse, another family member—to come to our rescue.

When we feel only one emotion, that's the one we act on, but it may not be the best way to handle the situation. Scolding our parents for soiling themselves only humiliates them. A better response is to help them get clean, then search for new solutions to the problem.

Other times, we may feel many emotions at once. The situation, however, may require that we set our emotions aside temporarily. In a medical emergency, for example, we need to appear calm, regardless of how alarmed we are.

Penny said, "When I'd enter the hospital, my heart would start pounding because I was afraid of what I might see, and I would feel guilty that I wanted this to be over with, but when I got to my father's room, I'd be relieved that he was still there, yet close to tears because his condition was so distressing. Then I'd try to hide my concern and say as nonchalantly as I could, 'Hi, Dad, you're looking good today.'"

Learning how to keep our emotions separate from the situation is not easy. Many caregivers seek the advice of a therapist as they begin to sort things out. Every caregiving situation is unique, but we can approach most crises by taking care to focus on the problem first.

Because the situation may be different from what it appears to be, it's best to make sure we have all the facts before we make any decisions. We can look, listen, and ask before we act. What do we see? What are we being told? Do we need advice, clarification? What is the appropriate action?

Once we have addressed the problem, we can focus on ourselves—reviewing what we did, how we felt about it, and whether or not our response was the best one under the circumstances.

## RIGIDITY VERSUS FLEXIBILITY

One of the clues to how we're handling our role as caregiver is whether we are rigid or flexible in the way we handle our duties. When our thinking is rigid, new suggestions become offensive. Any disagreement with what we believe creates an intolerable dissonance within ourselves. An opposing point of view annoys us. We say, "How dare he suggest . . ." or, "What does she know?" or, "It will never work." We dismiss any information that might force us to question ourselves. We only want outside information that agrees with us. We find it difficult to change our role or let others help us. We find ourselves "doing it all."

Vickie complained about all the attention her father required. "I stop by every evening on my way home from work so I can change his sheets, do a load of wash, feed the cat, and fix his dinner." Although her sister went on alternate evenings to attend to these same chores, Vickie stopped by anyway. "I just feel like I have to be there. She doesn't do things the way I like."

If we're flexible, we can accept that other points of view have merit. We're willing to act on a new suggestion, or at least give it a try. Being flexible means we can adapt, changing our caregiver role as needed and letting others participate as well. We understand that good caregiving requires diplomacy, outside support, and a practical network of assistance.

Being flexible means that negative thoughts and positive actions can coexist. We can continue our caregiving, even when we're upset and tired. We can do what needs to be done, even when we thought we couldn't. We bathe our parents, change their diapers, give them shots, wipe away sputum, all the while ignoring their accusations that we're stealing from them, abandoning them, taking advantage of them. We learn to do the best we can, even when we really don't want to.

It's not always easy to set our personal feelings aside in order to do what needs to be done. But when we can step outside of ourselves, our attitude begins to change. We begin to see how exhausting our parents' lives have become and how much they depend on others just to get through each day. Our resentment and guilt are replaced by sadness. Despair and fear are replaced by love. As difficult as our caregiving duties can be at times, we feel grateful that we are available to help our parents. Even if our parents can't acknowledge us, we know in our hearts that our presence gives them solace and comfort.

## CORE VALUES

It may help us as caregivers if we take time to reflect on our core values. These are the values and beliefs that we hold dear, the principles that we use to define our caregiving. We can then turn each value into a deed, a concrete commitment. The specific actions we take will vary from caregiver to caregiver, but the determination to be true to our core values will be the same.

It is important that we define these principles for ourselves, rather than let our parents, or anyone else, define them for us. Our caregiving commitment should come from our hearts, not from another's needs, guilt, or demands.

Our list of core values enables us to determine what we have to do in order to feel good about ourselves as caregivers. We can take a daily or weekly inventory to see that we are honoring our commitment to ourselves as well as to our parents. We can make sure that our walk matches our talk—that we're turning our words into actions. When our caregiving has ended, we can look at ourselves in the mirror and say, "I did the best that I was able to do."

Chuck's parents have many debts. Rather than give them spending money, he decided to pay for their health insurance. "It is important to me that they have good medical care," he said.

Scott wants to know that his parents' possessions are being maintained properly, so he gives them one Saturday a month. On that day, he takes their list of jobs that need to be done and tries to do as many as he can. "Last month I painted the back door, had the furnace checked for the winter, and put on the storm windows."

The point is that we can choose to behave in a way that is right for us. We can make a commitment that is appropriate for us. In some families, our commitment might include some limits as well.

Sheryl said, "I will drop everything in an emergency and do whatever needs to be done. But I allow myself to decide what's a crisis and what's not. Mom being rushed to the hospital is an emergency. Mom calling me to say she has an important letter that has to be rushed to the post office is not."

We also need to think about what we want to accomplish. If we are hoping for a change in the relationship, the change will have to come from us. It is not realistic to expect that our parents will change. Any change has to start and end within ourselves. We have to be honest, asking ourselves whether we are dealing from compassion or fear or manipulation.

We become caregivers to honor our parents, and sometimes to honor ourselves. Ethan said, "I had to take my father in because otherwise he would have ended up on skid row. I couldn't live with myself if I had let that happen."

Still, we need to realize that there will be many times when we are living on just our internal sense of honor. There may be no other acknowledgment than what is in our own hearts. Every single day it's up to us to affirm the decision to do what we're doing. There may never be any affirmation or recognition from the rest of the family.

Once we're the designated caregivers, it will be difficult to ignore family expectations. Maybe we decide that this year we're not going to host the family for the holidays. Or we're going to be out of town on Grandma's birthday. Or we're going to stop by twice a week instead of every day.

The reaction is likely to be stern, swift, and negative. "You have abandoned [me] [them] [us]." "You're not taking care of [me] [them] [us]." "This is a betrayal." "You're so selfish." "We always thought we could count on you."

Our first reaction is to defend our position. We explain, clarify, appeal, describe, and plead for understanding, but we can't win. Our reasons have no meaning to other family members. They're not caregivers, so they don't know what's involved, and further, they're not interested in knowing. They minimize what we do, saying, "What's the big deal?" "Stop whining." "Don't be such a martyr."

Finally we learn that it's best to keep our own counsel. We say, "Here's what I can do," and then we do it. We don't explain, justify, or rationalize. We choose what we feel is right, and we act accordingly.

When the situation is overwhelming, we sometimes question why we're doing this. Our parents are crazy and the rest of the family is nuts. Nobody appreciates what we're doing. Nobody gets it. Nobody understands. We ask ourselves why we continue to take care of our parents, why we don't turn our backs.

Each of us has a personal answer. Alex said, "I feel a moral obligation to take care of my mother. She's a piece of work, but she's still my mom."

Lois said, "I stay because this is the way I have chosen to honor my parents. I don't have to like them. I'm not even sure I love them. But I do choose to honor them by taking care of them."

# III

# TIME FOR ACTION

## CHOICES AND COMPROMISES

# SEVEN

## FINDING A NEW ROLE

One of our biggest challenges as caregivers is to create a new role for ourselves within our family of origin. We'll still be caregivers, we'll still do what has to be done, but we can learn to react differently, challenging our family role and making our expectations match reality. We can change, even if no one else in the family will. We can look for outside help, examine all available choices, adjust our priorities to include our own lives, and set boundaries where we need them. In the process, we will do more than become better caregivers. We will learn to honor ourselves.

Many of us have received honors in our other roles. We may have served our country or achieved success in our careers. We may be recognized as leaders in our communities. We may be known as loyal friends. Even if we're considered gurus in other areas, when it comes to our parents, enlightenment may go out the door. Our most trying relationships are often with our parents, so when we become their caregivers, assuming a new role for ourselves will not be easy. Yet if we are not careful, we will remain stuck in the past, reliving old roles and rigid behavior.

It's time for us to come to the caregiving role with a new

attitude. We can make a deliberate decision—we're here, we're doing it, so we are going to claim it. This may not be an easy decision, particularly when we feel our parents were not all that committed to caring for us. Still, making a commitment to care for them can empower us.

In claiming our role as caregiver, we're allowing ourselves the freedom to make decisions and set boundaries. We're ready to stop fighting with them and ourselves, accepting that we can balance our feelings with our commitment. We can say, "Here's the situation and here's what I'm going to do. I'm going to take care of my parents. I am the responsible person in a family with [no other] [not enough] [inadequate] caregivers. Now, how do I want to do this? How am I going to do my best and be equally conscious of my other responsibilities?"

## EXPECTATIONS

Finding a new role often means changing our expectations. What do we expect from ourselves? From others? What do we think the rest of the world expects from us? Which expectations do we honor? Which ones do we let go?

We need to think about the expectations we put on ourselves. Laura said, "My mother used to tell me how she sacrificed her life for me, how she didn't have any fun, any free time, and all that. So when I was taking care of her, I started to do the same thing. I began to think, *If I'm going to be worthy, then this is the way it's supposed to look. Caregiving is supposed to be one sacrifice after another.*"

We have to set our own rules about what makes us a good caregiver. If we trust ourselves and listen to our inner voices, we will know what is reasonable for us to do. We can trust ourselves to decide what is right and proper, not Mom and

Dad, not our peers, not society. The way caregiving looks is the way we decide it will look.

Our expectations about other people should be realistic. Are other family members really going to do their share, or are they going to complain and carry on so much that we wish we'd never asked? Are they ever going to change? Do they appreciate our efforts, or do they even care very much about what we do? Will they care for Mom and Dad the way we want them to?

What's important is not the answers, but our expectations. Once our expectations match reality, we no longer have to be surprised, disappointed, or resentful. Terry said, "I had to quit waiting for my brother to do his share. Now that I expect the obvious—I know he'll do next to nothing—I no longer waste my energy getting upset about it."

When we have expectations that are realistic, we can keep a more balanced view of the situation. If family members are difficult to deal with, we no longer expect that they will listen to reason, now or ever. If people need to change, we no longer expect that we can make it happen. Finally, we face our caregiving duties with open eyes. We will continue to do what we can to improve our parents' living conditions and, we hope, bring some stability to their lives, but the reality of the aging process means that no improvement will be permanent.

## CHOICES

Being a caregiver is not something we automatically know how to do. Few of us had any positive models for caregiving, so it becomes a role we have to carve out for ourselves.

Caregiving is hard; it is never an easy experience. If our relationship with our parents is difficult or even dysfunctional, we need to understand that caregiving probably won't fix it. Ken said, "I don't get along very well with my mom, so it's been difficult taking care of her. She makes me so crazy sometimes that I want to run screaming into the next room and start throwing dishes."

No matter what our particular situation is, we always have choices. We can choose whether to accept the role of caregiver. We can choose not to replay the family dysfunctions. We can choose to find a healthier way to manage the problems that arise. We can choose whether to maintain our own freedom at the same time. The freedom comes when we can act within our own definition, rather than doing what was chosen for us by somebody else.

There are a number of things that limit the choices available to us. To start with, we may not even realize that we have choices. But we do—our choices might be slim, but choices are there. In spite of our parents' decline, in spite of the family dysfunction, we still have choices about how to deal with the caregiving.

If our parents have limited financial resources, we can choose to look for financial assistance from outside agencies. We may decide to chip in ourselves, if we can do so without putting our own financial stability in jeopardy.

Sometimes we lose sight of our choices because we're so busy looking outside ourselves. We blame our parents, our siblings, the world. If "they" would do more, if "they" would cooperate, if "they" would look at what this is doing to us, and on and on. Once we stop blaming others, however, we empower ourselves. We choose to help the best way that we can. We concentrate only on our own caregiving responsibilities, not anyone else's.

It's no longer a matter of brother John refusing to visit Dad. It is "John won't be visiting today, so here are my choices."

It's no longer a matter of "Mom doesn't want anybody to help her but me." It is "Mom needs help, and here are choices that work for both of us."

The kind of help we need may not be available in our area. For example, if our parents are unable to live alone and we cannot find competent or trustworthy people to live with them, the option of live-in help is not available. We have to consider other possibilities, such as an assisted-living facility, a nursing home, or having our parents live with us.

Our choices might be limited because we don't live near our parents. Since we are unable to check on them as often as we would like, we might want to look for a geriatric care manager in the local area to assist them. Or we may decide it's a good idea to move our parents closer to us.

If our parents are not lucid, their mental helplessness limits the options we have in caring for them. For example, communication may be difficult or impossible. They can't share their needs and feelings with us, and we don't know how to soothe their fears.

Heather said, "My mother had Alzheimer's, and we finally had to put her in a nursing home. It took her a long time to adjust to the new surroundings. It was heartbreaking because she was so terrified. She had the look of a deer in the headlights."

Our choices are especially hard when our parents have diminished mental capacities, but not consistently so. Roxanne described her mother's early signs of dementia, "One day she thinks she is at someone else's house. The next day, she knows exactly where she is."

What we are really doing at this stage of caregiving is making choices and compromises at the same time. Certainly we are trying to make better choices than we once did. We're trying to be more flexible, more open to other opinions. But we are also making compromises because of the limits put on us by family dynamics.

Julie's father is very stubborn and headstrong. She is convinced that he would be better off and even happier in a different living situation, but he refuses to discuss other options. She said, "I finally had to stop talking about it. I don't like his current arrangement, but as long as it's not harmful, I guess it will have to do."

Caregiving is about the choices that are available to us and about what we do with the choices we have. Finding a new role means we are looking for the most positive choices available. We are willing to get creative. We are striving to add as much value to the caregiving situation as we can. We are learning to create freedom for ourselves, even as we attempt to bring peace and comfort to our parents.

## PRIORITIES

When we're in the middle of a caregiving crisis, we put everything on hold while we take care of the emergency. This is fine, as long as we're clear on what is an emergency and what isn't. If we're not careful, we'll suddenly realize that we've let every caregiving moment take priority over ourselves, our children, our spouse, our job. We feel exhausted, overwhelmed, burned out. We've lost sight of why we're doing all this, and we wonder how much longer we can maintain the pace.

Good caregiving means we set priorities. We accept that we can't do it all, but we can do what's important. And further, we can decide for ourselves what is important.

It's important that we take care of ourselves. We can eat right, walk every day, stop using tobacco, alcohol, and other mind-altering substances. We can try to get a good night's sleep. We can maintain a regular routine more days than not.

We can pay attention to the needs of our spouse and children. Dinner around the kitchen table gives everyone a chance to be heard and feel important. We can listen attentively as our children share the events of their day. We can set aside an evening to be alone with our spouse. We can attend local events as a family, such as a high school football game or county fair.

Balancing the demands of our job along with our family responsibilities is never easy. Rhonda carries a pager so her mother can contact her at work. She said, "No one else has to know she's paging me. It's much better than having someone interrupt a meeting to say my mother called again. This way she knows I'll call her as soon as I can."

At the same time, caregivers often find that work offers a mental respite from the demands of our parents. Vera said, "When I'm teaching, I'm in another world. I deal with caregiving when I get home."

### BEING TAKEN FOR GRANTED

Finding a new role means we look inward for approval. Having our parents or relatives say what a good job we're doing might never come to pass. More likely, our parents and siblings take us for granted because we're there. Their attitude seems to be, "Caregiving is your problem. You took it on; you deal with it." In fact, sometimes families have excessive expectations of the caregiver, making us feel guilty that we're not doing enough.

It is not uncommon for seniors to tell their friends and relatives what poor care we're giving them. They might say we are ungrateful, uncaring, and unloving. "After all we have done," they say, "our children have abandoned us in our hour of need."

Kathleen said, "I was helping my mother pack boxes and

get ready to move. One day she looked at me and said, 'Sandra [next-door neighbor] would never treat her mother this way.'"

Our first response is to want to defend ourselves to everyone, but a better response is to look in the mirror and reassure the person we see. "You are doing a good job; you are giving it your best."

When we can praise ourselves, we free ourselves. The old weapon of withholding approval is no longer effective. We no longer expect it; we no longer need it. We can thank ourselves for being a good caregiver. We can thank our friends for telling us what a good job we're doing. And in the end, we can feel sorry that our parents were too dysfunctional to tell us what we know was in their hearts.

### SETTING BOUNDARIES

What our boundaries are depends on the history of our relationship with our parents. We can set boundaries about many things, for example, alcohol consumption, noise levels from the stereo, late-night visitors. The issue is not the particular boundaries but whether they are respected, and in some cases, whether we even know that we have a right to set boundaries.

What makes this difficult is that there is still that young child inside us who has been trained to obey Mom and Dad. Before we know it, we are jumping through the old childhood hoops again. Our parents are aging and frightened. They want us there all the time. Their needs are so great that their concern is only for themselves. They become inwardly focused, unaware of anyone else's problems but their own. They no longer understand that we have other obligations in our lives—our job, our children, our spouse, ourselves. Now that we're adult caregivers, we're trying to set boundaries with sick parents, dysfunctional family members, and ourselves—people who weren't all that good with boundaries in the first place.

One of the problems with caregiving is how to compartmentalize what we have to do, yet protect ourselves at the same time. Certain caregiving duties mean that privacy flies out the window. Our parents need help bathing, managing their toileting needs, getting dressed. We discover that we're doing things for them physically that we can barely manage emotionally. We expected to assume this type of responsibility for our children, but not our parents. When the parent-child boundary is reversed, we feel like the natural order of the universe has been turned inside out.

Rita said, "I was cleaning up my mother, leaning behind her over the toilet. I didn't want to embarrass her, but it was all I could do not to gag from the mess and odor."

George said, "I can empty my dad's urinal, but I can barely deal with his false teeth. I have to put on gloves and look the other way just to hand them to him in a cup."

It's when we're going beyond what we feel we can do that we start to feel resentful. We resent our parents for no longer being able to care for themselves, and we resent what we now have to do for them. Our caregiving duties start to feel unfair. We wonder how we're going to protect ourselves while we try to find a way to do what needs to be done.

The answer is to listen to ourselves. When we ignore our inner voice, when we fail to pay attention to the boundaries that we need, our resentment starts to build. It makes no difference what another person decides to do—or not do—as a caregiver. We can only monitor our own feelings, our own choices.

Being a caregiver for our parents carries with it a certain

amount of resentment that probably won't completely disappear. We may not be able to erase that feeling, but we can do much to minimize it. We can use that feeling as a gauge to measure whether we've crossed an internal boundary line. When we feel a strong level of resentment, we can use that as a cue that we need to step back and reexamine what we're doing. We can take another look to see whether there are alternative solutions that allow us to solve the problems without crossing the boundaries that trigger our resentment.

Attacking and berating our parents does neither them nor us any good. In our frustration, we say, "Can't you see what you are doing to me?" The answer is no, they cannot understand the implications of their demands.

Our goal is to set boundaries with which we are comfortable, limits that we can enforce without an explanation. However, we want to do this with a kind, gentle, and positive voice. We can say, "I can see that you are very upset with me, so I will come back later when things have calmed down" or, "I know you are disappointed, but I will not be available to you tomorrow."

Irene lives with her mother and a full-time caregiver. While she is at work, her mother is content, but the minute she returns home, Mom begins to worry that her daughter will leave again. Irene said, "Usually I stay home, but if I want to go out again, it's just easier to say I have to go back to work. Mom has lost her sense of time, so that reason is okay with her. I think of it as a therapeutic lie."

Vacations can be a problem for caregivers. Our parents are nervous when we're out of town, so we promise to call frequently, hoping to ease their anxiety. Yet caregivers are often in desperate need of uninterrupted time alone.

Stephanie said, "Whenever I called my parents, there was always a problem to solve. It ruined my vacation because it was like having them in the trunk of the car. This year I gave them my itinerary in case of an emergency, but I didn't call until I got back home."

When overwhelmed, many caregivers will turn to other family members. If we expect them to help, we may be crushed with disappointment when they don't. But if we say that they "should" do this or that, we're talking about our own expectations—our boundaries, not theirs. In the same way, what they think we "should" do has to do with their idea of what caregiving means, not ours. It's about their relationship with our parents and has nothing to do with us.

We need to find our own emotional center, our own place of spiritual balance, then live within that space. Each of us has to set our own limits and be comfortable with our own boundaries. We have to concentrate on ourselves and be willing to let go of what others do. Our job is to stay centered, not to pass judgment.

## DEALING WITH OUR SIBLINGS

When we first began our caregiving journey, we probably told ourselves and our friends how cooperative our brothers and sisters were, how we all got along so well, and how everyone promised to do their share. The reality is very often the opposite. Some of us are going to pitch in and some of us are not. We discover that we don't get along because we never really did. What was true then is true now.

Our first reaction is most likely frustration and resentment. If we want to move away from that, however, we have to step back and think about our siblings when they were younger. We need to look at the relationships that we and our siblings had with each other as well as the relationship each sibling had with our parents.

If a sibling is still emotionally tied to a difficult episode from the past, we may be tempted to say, "Get over it." It is easy for us to say, but it may be hard for them to do. Getting over something is up to them, not us.

We need to accept that our siblings are going to do whatever it is they are going to do. No matter how much we rant or rave, they are not going to do more or do less. It may very well be that our siblings are not going to change at all. Again, we have to remember that we can only change ourselves. We cannot control their words or actions. We can only control how we think, what we say, and what we choose to do.

It may help us to understand our siblings better if we ask them what it was like for them when such-and-such happened. We need to honor each sibling's recollection, even if it is different from our own. Our parents may have presented a different side of themselves to our siblings, or each sibling may have experienced the same event differently simply because of his or her age at the time. Our goal is to understand our siblings, not judge them. The more we understand how they think, the more we are going to accept what they can do in terms of taking care of our parents. We may not agree with the choices our siblings make. We can only accept that they have made those choices.

It is not at all unusual for the adult children in a family to disagree on the decisions that have to be made on behalf of the parents. Our parents may try to engage the distant siblings by complaining about our lack of care. In addition, each sibling may have a separate personal agenda, such as guilt, compassion, resentment, or even larceny.

Typically, the siblings who are most removed tend to retreat into denial. Their physical or emotional distance makes it easier for them to ignore the changes in their parents' behavior or the increase in their parents' demands and needs.

These siblings are not happy to hear that big changes are occurring. They may find it hard to believe, especially if our parents put their best foot forward when the out-of-town siblings come home for a visit.

Inheritance issues often come to light when the family is under stress. We may not approve of what other family members are doing, but it is not our job to criticize or control. It is our job to be appropriate and ethical. We want to treat our parents, their money, and their possessions the same way we treat our friends and peers and their money and possessions. When legal or financial affairs need resolution, we can contact an attorney or accountant.

At the same time, we need to be aware of the limitations of our family system. No matter how confident we feel about our point of view, our opinion may not be the one that prevails. We have to be prepared to step back and be out-voted.

We should also bear in mind that our caregiving days will not last forever. After our parents are gone, we and our siblings will be all that's left of our original family. Mom and Dad will no longer be there to keep us apart or keep us together. The way we behave with one another in the caregiving situation can affect our attitudes toward one another for many years to come. We don't have to overlook inappropriate behavior just because it is within the family. At the same time, being a caregiver doesn't entitle us to act that way either. Our task is to bring integrity to the caregiving process, using it as a way to build our inner strength, not deplete it.

## CREATING FREEDOM

We can set our own rules about what makes us a good caregiver, a good child, a good sibling, so that we won't feel guilty later on. As we let go of old roles, we can learn to attend to the relationships in our lives that are important to us. We will be living with our spouse and children, our siblings and friends, long after our parents are gone. When we nurture them, we nurture ourselves.

In a sense, we are reprogramming ourselves. This is not easy to do because we are setting new boundaries with our parents, new rules for ourselves. We're crossing over from the old to the new. We have to remember that the only thing that is authentic to each of us is our own personal experiences. When we feel guilty, we know we are doing something wrong, but much of the time, we don't know how else to do it. Trying something new makes us feel different, hesitant, anxious. We're on unsure ground. We can see that redefining our role is going to require a great deal of attention.

We can start by clarifying our role as caregiver, taking time to think about our priorities, our choices, our boundaries, our expectations. What we can and will do varies from person to person, simply because our experiences are so different. We set our own parameters about what we are willing to do, the amount of time we have available, and what is appropriate or not appropriate for ourselves. We must also respect the parameters that other members of our family will set. Whether or not we agree is irrelevant. Our concern should be only with ourselves, our spouse, our children. We have to let go of what other family members think of us. We have to let go of what we think society expects of us.

Most of us want to do the best we can in caring for our parents. We are willing to make considerable sacrifices on their behalf; however, it is up to us to decide at what point caregiving becomes too toxic, too wearing, or too high a price to pay in the rest of our lives. We may not have been given the tools to do this, but because we are adults and have resources available to us, we can give these tools to ourselves.

Each crisis requires its own decision, and we handle these crises one at a time. At the same time, we are learning to recognize old messages from our youth, discarding those that are inappropriate. We are learning to trust and respect what is true for us. We are beginning to listen to our hearts.

# EIGHT

## DECISIONS AND PLANS

Providing care for our parents is all about working around obstacles and making compromises. The obstacles are the limitations we have to work with, the things that are in our way—perhaps a limited amount of money, family members that don't get along, a lack of outside help, or parents who are depressed or demented or difficult. The plan we come up with is going to be the result of one compromise after another.

One of the hardest parts of caregiving is realizing there are no perfect choices. What we want is to make our parents strong, give them health and vigor, restore their youth, give them a life. Those choices are no longer available. No matter what we do, our parents are going to leave this earth. Old age is an incurable disease.

We sometimes lose sight of the fact that nothing is permanent. What works today may not work tomorrow. Today we can read the telephone book; tomorrow we need glasses. Today Mom is confidently living alone; next week she's debilitated by a stroke and requires nursing-home care.

What is a good choice for one family may be just the opposite for another. Some caregivers want their parents to live with them; others say, no way. Sometimes even our parents have opposing ideas. Teresa said, "My mother really wanted to move into an assisted-living facility for seniors. My father, however, was adamant that they stay at home with live-in help." The choices we make are perhaps the best available, but even so, we feel as if we've had to make some major compromises and every choice is something of a concession.

What we're left with is trying to make the best choice under the circumstances, realizing that none of the choices available will solve the problem of old age. In the long run, the best we're going to do is make our parents safe, comfortable, and secure. A permanent cure—infinite health and life—isn't possible.

Many of us will also have to face the problem of our parents' living arrangements, another set of less-than-ideal choices. We can move them to a long-term care facility, hire live-in help, have them move in with us, or leave them on their own in spite of their infirmities. The choice we want— independence forever—is not on the list. No matter what we do, they're not going to get better. And we're going to feel like we've failed.

## MAKING DECISIONS

Eldercare decisions are never easy, especially when it comes to changing our parents' living arrangements. Most parents resist change, and caregivers understand why this is so. Nonetheless, there are times when difficult choices must be presented. Caregivers may have the best of intentions, the best information, and a clear picture of how to make both parents' and caregivers' lives more pleasant. The more dysfunctional the family, however, the less likely anyone will act. At the same time, family spectators may be quick to second-guess the caregiver and occasionally even interfere, offering unsolicited opinions and taking sides.

It is important to remember that eldercare crises rarely happen overnight. Many of the problems have been creeping up for a long time. Carol's parents are both in their eighties, and her father recently had a stroke. Her father requires a great deal of attention, but her mother insists on caring for him alone, saying, "I don't want a stranger in my house." Carol predicts that until her mother "falls over in a heap," she will continue to refuse all offers of help.

It is very hard when we have no emotional support from our immediate families. We feel alone with the responsibility, yet if we have no authority to make changes, our hands are tied. In the end, caregivers have to compromise, and sometimes the compromise is to let go. If there's no support for what we think should be done, we reluctantly may have to let go of certain choices and opportunities. We are forced to sit back, be quiet, and watch the train leave the tracks.

### RELIABILITY: WHO IS SAYING WHAT

Many caregivers find it surprising that their parents are no longer a reliable source of information, particularly regarding their health. Walter's mother was quite crippled with arthritis but insisted, "The doctor said I'm fine." Walter was taken aback because at the time his mother was barely able to walk.

When we hear unusual reports, we need to consider the source. The only way to know what the doctor really said is to ask the doctor. There might be a difference between what the doctor said and what our parent heard.

Raymond's father said, "The doctor said it's okay to take an extra two pills a day for my nerves." When Raymond checked with the doctor, the instructions were "one pill at night, only as needed."

To ensure good medical care, it is important to have a positive rapport with our parents' primary care physicians. A good relationship starts with adult children being objective about their parents' future. We can ask questions and educate ourselves about the condition that has incapacitated our parents. We can do what we can to ensure compliance at home regarding medications, hygiene, nutrition, and safety. We can make sure that every doctor treating our parents is made aware of prescriptions and treatment regimens from other medical specialists.

If we are not comfortable with one doctor, we can find another. If we are uneasy about a diagnosis or suggested treatment, we can seek a second opinion. Threatening legal action usually doesn't do any good. In fact, it generally ensures that more attention will be paid to liability issues than medical care.

We can be observant, seeing if what our parents say matches what they really do. We need to make sure that sufficient and accurate information is available to the doctor in the first place. It often falls to the caregiver to report symptoms and behaviors that are significant, including any past or present problems with addiction.

The prescribed drug for Roberta's mother had to be taken every eight hours around the clock. The timing was critical to avoid serious side effects. But Roberta knew her mother's pattern—take a dose, forget a dose, take a double dose in twelve hours, and so on—and explained the problem to the doctor. Armed with this information, the doctor changed drugs, choosing one that could be taken once a day, a regimen that her mother could follow.

Phil's father was so fearful of hearing bad news that he offered no information. "The doctor didn't ask me about my hip, so it must be okay," he said. Alison, on the other hand, described her mother as a hypochondriac, "symptoms in search of a disease." Alison tried to be observant and objective so she could help the doctor determine which of her mother's many symptoms were noteworthy.

In dysfunctional families, there are often secrets that set up another blockade to good medical treatment. Dr. T., an internist, said that adult children will sometimes report a parent's negative, covert behavior, such as "Dad is drinking again" or "Mom is still eating lots of sugar," then add, "but don't let on I told you." This puts the doctor in a difficult position because there may be no obvious reason to confront the patient. If the caregiver is present, however, the doctor can say, "Your [son] [daughter] is concerned about this."

There are many reasons why we back away from dealing with our parents' secret behavior directly. Chances are, we have never discussed the problem with our parent, so we have no idea where or how to begin. Or we may decide that our parent is too old, too addled, too confrontational to face by ourselves. Or we hope an outside authority will have influence that we don't. Maybe our parents will change their ways or be less resistant if someone outside the family talks to them.

Lee said, "My mother was a closet drinker and had bottles stashed all over the house. It was a forbidden topic when I was a kid, sort of like the elephant in the living room that nobody notices."

In avoiding a dispute with our parents, perhaps we're also avoiding the possibility that even if we confront our parent, nothing will change. Randy said, "I knew my father's smoking was killing him, but there was nothing we could do because he didn't want to quit. When he finally did, the damage was already done. He really quit too late."

Grace said, "My father died at forty-nine of alcoholism, but he never stopped drinking. He said, 'I can quit any time I want to.' If he wouldn't stop, the doctor couldn't do anything."

## GETTING SIBLINGS TO HELP

Caregivers often complain that their siblings aren't doing enough. Our perspective may have merit, and then again, it may not. We need to recognize that our siblings may have valid reasons for what they choose to do, and in some cases, they simply don't know how to help. The real issue is that the situation probably won't change.

We've already discovered that dropping hints or complaining to our siblings gets us nowhere. In our frustration, we pour on the guilt and create even more resistance. Positive approaches usually work best. We can acknowledge their excuse, whether we agree with it or not. Then, rather than complain, we can give specific suggestions. "Here are three things that need to be done this week. Which ones can you work into your schedule?" We can ask them to help us research the illness that is plaguing Mom. Or mention that it would be helpful if they would call our parents once a week. Or perhaps they could contribute money toward the services that our parents need.

We have to expect that our siblings may want to do things in a different way than we do. We need to remember that different is not necessarily wrong. If we criticize, they are likely to say, "Do it yourself." We should also take care to thank them for whatever they do offer. It may not be very much, but it is worth something.

If we have siblings who live in a different part of the country, it's important that we keep them informed ourselves, as our parents may be giving them a different story. We need to be aware that even the most supportive siblings may not understand the gravity of the situation.

Brenda said, "I was shocked when my sister and brother called to say they were putting Dad in a nursing home. I just found it hard to believe that he had gotten to that point already. I said okay because they were the ones taking care of him, but I bought a plane ticket because I guess I needed to see for myself."

Unfortunately, some caregivers report that their siblings criticize them, yet refuse to participate. In those cases, there is little point in defending what we're doing. We can suggest that our siblings take on the responsibilities themselves, but they won't. In the end, we have to accept the family situation for what it is. If there's no support from the family, then we need to look for help elsewhere.

## CAREGIVING FROM A DISTANCE

When we live far from our parents, taking care of them includes additional problems. If our parents have been telling us on the phone that all is well and they are doing fine, we need to pay close attention when we visit them. It could be that they have been telling us what we want to hear and what they want to believe.

When we visit, we can gather clues as to how well they really are doing. For example, is there food in the house? Is the pantry stocked? If they don't drive, how are they getting groceries? If their refrigerator is empty—or full of spoiled food—we can assume they are not eating nutritious meals every day.

The condition of the house is another clue. Laundry that has piled up, unpleasant odors, and living quarters that haven't been dusted or vacuumed recently are indications that our parents need help with housekeeping chores. We can look on our parents' desk to get an idea of how well they are taking care of their bills. A pile of unopened mail is a sure sign that they need help with their finances.

As we look around, we should be aware of any changes that may have occurred since our last visit. There may be changes in our parents' behavior and appearance that signal mental deterioration or caregiver abuse.

Dorothy said, "My mother was always meticulous about her appearance. Her hair was not as neat as it used to be, and she didn't seem interested in getting to the beauty parlor once a week like she used to. These were big changes as far as I was concerned."

If we have not seen our parents in some time, we want to plan carefully to take advantage of the time that we're with them. Appointments with their doctor, attorney, banker, or other professionals can be scheduled to coincide with our visit. We can ask before we leave home whether there are any records or other paperwork that we need to bring with us.

It is important to plan time for pleasure too. This can be as simple as making sure that we take time to sit and talk and listen.

Mark said, "When I went to visit my father, we would sit on the screened-in porch every night and watch the cars go by. Sometimes we would talk; sometimes we would work crossword puzzles or read the paper. I think sitting there with him gave him as much pleasure as anything I ever did."

When the main reason for our trip home is to get help for our parents, we can make the visit more productive by doing our homework in advance. We can call social service agencies in their area to find out about the various services available. Once we're on the scene, we can follow up in person with those that offer the kind of help our parents need.

Many adult children have found it helpful to have a quali-fied, objective social worker evaluate the situation on their behalf. Those who have special training in geriatric needs are certified as geriatric care managers. We may find that with a few simple changes, our parents can continue living alone. Perhaps a phone with volume control and large, easy-to-read buttons will make a difference. Maybe we need to add a handrail along the stairs leading from the house to the garage.

We may also have to face the reality that our parents should no longer live alone. Perhaps they can no longer navi-gate the stairs safely, or they're unsteady on their feet, or the neighborhood is deteriorating, or they're no longer able to help each other. We may need to have someone with them part or full time. Or we may have to tackle the dreaded prospect of moving them to more suitable living quarters.

Carla said, "My mother was just too sick with cancer to cope any longer. She was unable to cook, and my dad didn't know how. She called and said she was sorry, but it was time for me to step in."

### HELPING THE PRIMARY CAREGIVER

Some of us are secondary caregivers. We may live farthest away, or job responsibilities make it easier for us to step back, or we're willing to defer to another. Whatever the rea-sons, the primary caregiver is not us—it's a brother or sister. And that sibling will need all the support we can offer.

Typically, those of us who live at a distance tend to think that the situation is probably better than it really is, especially if our parents are putting up a false front for us because we're not there all the time.

Keith said, "When my brother phoned, my mother would sit up in bed and be lively and talkative, all the while saying how she was just fine. The second she hung up, she would flop back on the pillow, close her eyes, and groan."

Judy said that whenever her brother visited, her mother liked to ride along for the return trip to the train station. "She would be chatty and cheerful until my brother got out of the car. Then dead silence. She wouldn't say another word. She had used all her energy putting up a good front for my brother."

Sometimes we feel that the caregiver sibling is hysterical and irrational. Paula said, "My sister gets panicky and scared very easily, so sometimes it's hard to know what's really going on." In those cases, we need to get the facts from a primary source. If our parent is in the hospital, we can talk to the nurses. We can call the doctor and ask questions. We can tap into our own resources for information about a syndrome or disease. We can visit our parents and see for ourselves.

We also may be subjected to visits and phone calls that are loaded with guilt and anger, all of it directed at us. We begin to ignore our caregiver sibling, assuming that everything said is suspect. *It can't be that bad,* we say to ourselves. *There's no reason for [sibling] to act that way or to say those things.*

As distant siblings, we need to respect the fact that the burden is not on us. It is on someone else. We cannot begin to understand the stress of week-in, week-out caregiving if we're not doing it. We also need to remember that our parents are only part of the story. Eldercare has a tremendous impact on the caregiver's life too.

Steve said, "My brother took care of my mother. He would complain bitterly that I didn't call often enough and I wasn't there to help. At first I would say, 'Don't give me a hard time.' But eventually I started to see something different. I actually started to see what it must be like from his point of view. I didn't like what he was turning into, but that didn't have anything to do with how it must be for him. So I started telling him that I understood how much it cost him emotionally to do what he was doing, and I acknowledged him and thanked him. It was authentic, not just me trying to be nice to him."

We can offer the primary caregiver some relief time when we visit, or we can take over for longer periods. Dana's two sisters used their vacation time to fill in for her after she had taken in their mother. Molly cared for her mother during the summer in order to give her sister a break.

We can try to put ourselves in our sibling's shoes, imagining what we might need if we were the primary caregiver. We can be direct, saying, "What can I do to help?"

We need to be aware that a senior's health can take a sudden and dramatic turn for the worse, and our parents may be much more frail than when we last saw them. Jessica said, "My mother had been healthy as could be, then she fractured her arm. One test led to the next, and suddenly the doctor is telling us that Mom's heart was bad and she wouldn't live another six months. I couldn't believe it."

Perhaps the best support we can offer is to listen and not judge. We can validate their efforts and be grateful that they're handling the situation. We can focus on them, not our parents, encouraging our siblings to take time out for themselves.

We can support the primary caregiver's decisions regarding our parents—after all, that's the person dealing with them all the time. Dennis said, "I told my brother that I would support everything he did where Mom was concerned. I didn't want to see her in a nursing home, but when my brother said the time had come, I didn't second-guess him."

Unfortunately, some distant siblings may have reason not

to trust the primary caregiver. We may feel that they are not paying enough attention, or they have competing motives, or they simply don't have the time or energy to keep a close watch on our parents. Berating the primary caregivers or giving them orders from afar is not the answer. They are doing the best they can, or at least what they choose to do. If we are not happy with what we see, our only choice is to assume primary responsibility ourselves.

## TALKING TO OUR PARENTS

Crisis management will be easier if we know ahead of time what our parents want us to do. It is one thing to carry out plans; it is quite another to initiate those plans. The sooner we talk to them about what to do when a catastrophe strikes, the better. It may help if we think of ourselves as partners with our parents. Partners share, listen, and make decisions together.

Certain topics such as financial and legal affairs, illness, and funeral arrangements are difficult to bring up. These are not easy conversations and there is never a good time to have them with our parents. When we do, we want to be as nonconfrontational as possible.

One way to bring up the topic is to share our own thoughts on these issues, then ask them for advice. For example, we can say that we are about to update our wills, then ask their opinion about different choices we are contemplating. After listening to their suggestions for us, we can easily direct the conversation to what they did for themselves.

We can also ask them about their fears, what concerns them the most. We can ask what we can do to lessen their worries and lighten their burden. We can reassure them that their worries can be addressed and offer suggestions for doing just that. In an ideal world, we would be able to have these discussions many years in advance of any crises. We would bring up the "what ifs" and our parents would tell us what to do.

It's always better if our parents make these decisions instead of us. If they refuse to talk about it, then any decisions are going to be made by us and other members of the family. What we decide might be quite different from what our parents would have chosen for themselves.

Discussing sensitive topics will stir up old issues. Even as we are talking to our parents, we have to look at our lives and feel what's in our hearts before we make a commitment we might not be able to honor. Perhaps our parents have said, "Promise you'll never put us in a nursing home." Our first inclination is probably to say, "I promise," even though we cannot foretell the future.

Valerie said, "I promised my parents I would look for other options first, but I also pointed out that in some circumstances, a nursing home might be the best choice. When I gave them specific examples, they were silent. They didn't want to hear that, but I know they did."

## BEING PREPARED

Caregivers need immediate and instant access to certain pieces of documentation. These include any advance directives from our parents, such as a living will and a copy of their healthcare power of attorney. If our parents have lived their lives in denial and chaos, these documents may not exist. It may be up to us to find a trusted person, such as an attorney, who can work with our parents to process these documents.

It's good to keep a copy of these documents in a purse,

briefcase, or glove compartment of the car. It is also a good idea to give a copy of these documents to the hospital as part of our parents' permanent medical records. Once the paramedics are at the scene or we are hovering in the emergency room, it is not enough to say, "I know what Mom wants, but I don't have the papers with me."

Doreen said, "My mother had a heart attack about a week after she had given me healthcare power of attorney. Unfortunately, I was at her house and the power of attorney was at my house. So my mother was resuscitated and her life was saved, but I am not sure whether it did her any good. She was very unhappy about it, and the last two years of her life were miserable. There was no quality of life at that point."

It is also a good idea to keep a list of important phone numbers on hand at all times. Most caregivers discover that they can handle any emergency by phone even if they are far away and unable to reach the scene. The list should include the names and numbers of doctors, the pharmacy, hospital emergency room, and closest relative. We can plan by imagining a "worst case" scenario and prepare our list accordingly. We might want to include phone numbers for attorney, funeral home, and key friends and relatives.

Another way to put everyone's minds at ease is to carry a pager or cell phone. That way, our parents can reach us night and day, even if we're on vacation. We should expect, however, that if we are the primary caregivers, our parents and family members will want us to handle a crisis in person. It's up to us to decide whether it's necessary to return immediately.

# NINE

## LIVING ARRANGEMENTS

It's inevitable that living arrangements become an issue as we watch our parents become less and less able to care for themselves easily or effectively. Ideally, of course, our parents have been willing to discuss alternate housing arrangements before any medical crisis arises, but the reality is usually the opposite. That leaves the caregivers to step forward and start the process of deciding what kind of living situation might be best. What everyone—parents and siblings—wants is independence, but that is no longer possible. They are too weak, too befuddled, too incapacitated, too dependent to live alone any longer.

Any change of living arrangements is a difficult decision and will have an impact on all members of the family, caregivers as well as aging parents. The more we can discuss these issues in advance of a crisis, the better. We need to make sure that all family members, even grandchildren, have a chance to express their feelings before a final decision is made.

Our choices are essentially two: bring help to our parents or take them to where help is available. There is probably no ideal choice at this point. All we can do is try our best to see that our parents are receiving appropriate attention each day. Although some of our burden will be lifted, we need to accept that while we address one issue, we may very well be creating another. Depending on how our parents adapt to change, these issues will be either minimized or made worse.

These transitions will be easier if the caregivers are merely carrying out a decision our parents made when they were of sound mind. Fred said that although his parents resisted these changes at the end of their lives, he recalled them telling him ten years earlier that they would trust him to do what was in their best interest. "I really felt that the decision had been theirs, not mine," he said. "All I was doing was making it happen."

To the extent possible, it is best if our parents are part of all discussions and decisions regarding where they live. It is reasonable, and even necessary, that our parents be present when we discuss options with other family members or get recommendations from outside professionals about what to do. Healthcare professionals can offer a great deal of assistance to seniors and their families. We can ask a social worker who specializes in geriatric care to come to our parents' home and evaluate their medical, physical, and social needs. When we are faced with difficult choices, we can let the healthcare professionals introduce these options to our aging parents and help them accept these choices.

Part of our discussion should include family issues. Evelyn said, "My father needed to be on a special diet, but my mother was no longer cooking. Any housing option for them had to include meals prepared by someone else."

Bill set up a meeting with the stroke rehabilitation staff and his father. One at a time, each staff member gave reasons why his father should no longer live alone. The result was that his father decided to hire live-in help. Bill knew that if he had presented the reasons, his dad would have accused his son of trying to control him. "By having the staff meet with him, he was made to feel that he was still in control," Bill said. "The transition was much easier simply because the decision came from him, not me."

Caregivers need a network of objective, qualified health-care professionals, including doctors, nurses, pharmacists, hospitals, social workers, clergy, counselors, and more. These people can offer guidance if we only ask. They will discuss options with us and offer recommendations. Their goal will be the same as ours: to help ensure that our parents are safe and that their healthcare needs are being met.

It is important to remember that there is no right answer—and no wrong answer. There is the opportunity to use functional problem-solving skills instead of reverting to the old dysfunctional tactics of controlling, reacting, shutting down, or leaving.

When we problem solve, we explore choices. There are choices that aren't available, choices that are rejected, choices that are dictated by circumstance, choices that the caregivers want, choices that the parents demand, and for better or worse, there is the choice that the family finally makes.

## HIRING TEMPORARY HELP

Most caregivers want to keep their parents at home, living independently, as long as possible. One way to keep them at home is to hire temporary help. We can hire someone to help with housecleaning, laundry, bathing, lawn maintenance, or other tasks of daily living. The biggest advantage, of course, is that occasional assistance will help our parents remain in their homes a bit longer. It will also make their day-to-day life easier.

Perhaps the biggest obstacle to overcome when hiring temporary help is simply convincing our parents that they need this extra assistance. There is also the problem of finding help. We can ask our friends for recommendations, call an agency, or check with a social service agency, but in many areas there is a shortage of qualified people.

Hiring temporary help also means a new expenditure. Our parents may have limited funds or may be worried that there won't be enough money to cover their expenses for the rest of their lives. In addition to money worries, many parents say, "I don't want a stranger in the house." In a dysfunctional family especially, this translates as the parents saying, "We want our adult children to do it."

Although temporary help will ease the burden on caregivers, we are still actively involved. We have to find help, hire help, and make sure that the job is being done.

### HIRING LIVE-IN HELP

The advantage of live-in help is that our parents still feel independent. They are in familiar surroundings, their own home, and the cost of taking care of them at home is generally less than it would be in a senior-housing situation. This is particularly true if both parents require assistance and care. The ratio of staff to patient is, of course, one to one or one to two.

Karen said, "Both of my parents were quite ill, too sick for any kind of assisted-living situation. We decided that rather than put them in a nursing home, we would bring the nursing home to them. So we hired live-in help. They got to stay at home, and it was less costly too."

There are disadvantages to live-in help. In many cases, the financial cost of live-in help is not covered by insurance, and it can be considerable. Many families have discovered that it is as difficult to find reliable live-in help as it is to afford it. As our parents become more and more housebound, they also become increasingly isolated. Their social skills decline, they become more narcissistic, less and less interested in anyone else.

An overlooked problem with live-in help is that in order to make the situation work, the live-in employee becomes part of the family. Over time, the boundaries between family and employee become very fuzzy. As our parents become more debilitated, they also become increasingly dependent on the person taking care of them all day. Our parents feel they "can't get along without" this person. This sets the stage for the employee to have a great deal of emotional control over our parents.

Curt said, "My dad was still signing [the live-in's] paycheck, so even though he wanted me to supervise the situation, I had no real authority. Whenever [the live-in] didn't like what I suggested, she would throw a hissy fit at my dad and he would tell me to back off."

Our live-in helpers also suffer burnout. Even under the best of circumstances, we need to expect that most will leave after a year or two. Kate said, "My mother is demented and very verbally abusive. She calls our helpers terrible names, swears at them. She's awful. No one will stay with her very long, and I can't say I blame them."

## SENIOR HOUSING

As the population of seniors becomes larger, there are more housing options available if our parents are willing to leave their home. These include independent living, assisted living, and nursing home living. The advantage is that these facilities are staffed to help our parents. Most offer housekeeping and laundry assistance, and meals are offered in a central dining room. This type of housing also offers our parents a social life. Interacting with other people their own age helps them maintain their social skills and behave appropriately for a longer period of time.

"Independent living" typically means each resident has a small apartment, including a kitchenette. Many seniors choose to prepare their own breakfast and lunch but have dinner in the dining room with everyone else. There may be a social director who plans outings and activities. Seniors in "assisted living" usually have their own rooms or suites but need help with the activities of daily living, such as getting dressed, bathing, and taking medications.

Call it what we will, senior housing is similar to dormitory living. It is not easy to find a good facility or one that is affordable. Our parents may see this choice as a loss of autonomy and privacy, and to some extent, it is.

Caregivers still need to visit often and be prepared to advocate for their parents. Janice said, "I moved my parents three times before I found the right place. What I finally had to do was separate them. Now he's in an Alzheimer's facility and she is in independent living."

## NURSING HOMES

Nursing-home facilities provide intermediate or skilled nursing care. Intermediate care is for residents who are unable to walk or move without assistance, who need help getting dressed, and who may require daily medications that have to be administered by a nurse.

Patients needing skilled nursing care are typically very limited in their mobility, even bedfast or comatose, on respirators and feeding tubes, and more. Some patients also require skilled nursing care to recover after surgery or a debilitating illness.

Guilt and anguish go hand-in-hand with choosing a nursing home. We feel like we are "warehousing" our parents, yet they require more care than we can give them at home. In some cases, the emotional cost of long-term caregiving takes its toll, and a nursing home becomes a more palatable option than we once thought.

Dawn said, "After eleven years of caregiving, I was burned out. I just couldn't do it anymore. The stress was affecting my health, my marriage was in trouble, my kids were angry. It was too much."

Although a nursing home may ease the strain on the caregivers, we need to be aware that we're trading one set of problems for another. Nursing homes are notorious for being understaffed and poorly managed. There are far too many documented cases of physical, emotional, and sexual abuse. Good nursing-home care is hard to find and can be quite expensive. We will have to find financial assistance for our parents if they outlive their financial resources.

A nursing home will give the adult children some needed emotional distance, but we will still need to be advocates for our parents and actively involved in monitoring their care. Frank's mother was in a nursing home and had fallen three times, so he insisted his mother be moved to a different floor. "I wanted to keep her from suffering any injuries that she didn't have to suffer. I felt the nursing home was okay overall, but I knew the supervisor on her floor was not doing a good job. Once she was moved to a different wing, the problem was solved. An aide accompanied her whenever she was standing or walking."

### LIVING WITH ADULT CHILDREN

Many caregivers entertain the notion of having their parents move in with them. At first thought, it seems logical enough. Our parents can help us with chores, they'll conserve their money, they'll lavish attention on the grandchildren, and in a moment of weakness, we tell ourselves we'll enjoy their company.

This is the time to explore old family roles once again. If having our parents live with us plays into our need to control or please, it will open old wounds. If we are at risk of harming our parents, we need to seek other housing alternatives. We need to be aware that abuse of the elderly can be one of the dysfunctional responses to the stresses of caregiving.

One of the reasons we may want our parents to live with us is because we feel their home is no longer safe for them. But is our house any safer? We need to think about the location of bedrooms, bathrooms, and stairs in our house or apartment. If we need to make a few changes, what will it cost? If both adult child and spouse work outside the home, will we need to hire outside help to keep an eye on our parents?

Most important, we need to be realistic about future needs of our parents. If they can't live alone now, how much longer can they reasonably live with us? We need to think about the impact of their presence on us, on our spouse and children, on our ability to function at home and at work.

If our relationship with our parents is already strained, we needn't expect this to change. Living under the same roof is probably going to make it worse. They will be underfoot all the time, needy, annoying, demanding, and forgetful. They will be invading our space. We'll soon start treating them like children. How long will it be before we're resentful, irritable, and impatient? How long before our spouse is peeved, before our teenagers find excuses to avoid being at home?

We forget that in living with us, we're taking away our parents' privacy too. They will have no space, no territory to call their own. They will be the guests who overstay their welcome, yet they are too frail and feeble to leave—and if they have given up their own home or apartment, they no longer have any place to go.

Eric said, "I was thirty-seven when Mom died, so I had Dad move in with me. He lived with us for eleven years. There wasn't any other choice because he wasn't able to take care of himself. It was tough. He wasn't disruptive, but his behavior was often inappropriate. Like, for instance, he had no table manners. He would just shovel food in his mouth. It was disgusting to watch him eat. So finally we got to where we'd feed him first. He'd eat alone, but that didn't bother him. Then when he was done, my wife and the girls and I would eat together. That kind of stuff made family affairs difficult. You just never knew what the guy was going to say, so it was always, 'What are we going to do about Dad?'

"He was pretty demanding. 'Get me this' or 'I want that.' He never said thanks. Never. Not once. It was hard on my wife. Dad was a big problem for her. We tried behavior modification, everything we could think of. He was just totally self-absorbed. We had to keep after him to get up, get dressed, take a bath. Otherwise he'd just sit in his bathrobe in front of the TV all day.

"I would dream up stuff for him to do. One time I gave him all my tools and told him to clean them up. I had him scrape all the rust off and then paint everything. That kept him busy for a few weeks and out of trouble.

"As for taking care of my dad, it was hard. I did what I had to do, but I wouldn't judge another person for doing something different."

### RESPITE CARE

Sometimes mental health issues, such as Alzheimer's or other types of dementia, disable our parents. Even if they are physically able, we realize that they are no longer mentally competent to care for themselves without assistance.

Adult day care programs are very helpful to families who are facing these kinds of problems. They provide supervision and activities during the day to help keep the seniors alert and engaged with the world as long as possible. Most of these programs are careful to put participants into groups of equal abilities.

When round-the-clock attention is required, there are facilities that specialize in caring for demented adults. Some also offer short-term care so that families can take breaks, such as vacations, without worrying about their parents.

### ELDER ABUSE

Many of us assume that any abuse of our parents is most likely to happen in a nursing home, but according to the American Psychological Association, most cases of elder abuse happen at home.

In families where physical abuse was the norm, we may have been victims when we were children. What we need to realize is that as adults, we are at risk for repeating this behavior. We are more likely than most caregivers to harm our parents, abusing and neglecting them when we are frustrated, angry, and overwhelmed with caregiving chores. If this is the case, we will need to find another caregiver to replace us.

If we suspect our parents are being abused by another family member or other caregiver, it is imperative that we investigate the situation right away. Unexplained bodily injuries, torn underwear, genital bruises and bleeding, or a reluctance to seek medical treatment are often signs of physical or sexual abuse. Bedsores and excessive hunger or thirst can indicate neglect. Unreasonable fear, social isolation, or evasiveness suggest possible emotional abuse. A flurry of banking activity can signal financial exploitation. When we find abuse has taken place, we must take immediate steps to protect our parents.

### MAKING A PLACEMENT DECISION

As we try to make an appropriate decision regarding living arrangements for our parents, we need to look realistically at our entire family. We need to remember that as the needs of our parents increase, primary caregivers are affected too. We suffer more fatigue; we are less productive and often consumed with self-doubt and guilt. We ask ourselves, *Are we doing enough? Should we do more?* We start to put our lives and our health on hold in order to provide care for our parents.

We are also mourning the loss of the good things in our original relationship. We can no longer depend on Dad for advice about the garden. We can't ask Mom to help us finish that sweater because she doesn't remember how to knit anymore. The good feelings that we may have had no longer exist because of the changes in their personality or their physical and mental deterioration. This is particularly difficult if the good things about our relationship were few and far between. We had so little and now we are losing even that.

We have to ask ourselves whether the increased demands

on us are affecting the care we are giving our parents. If we're depressed, are we conveying that to our parents? Is our frustration making us short-tempered and impatient with them? Further, the question is not only what can we do to improve our parents' situation, but in fact, can the situation improve? It may be that both the parents' and the caregiver's needs are too much to be going it alone anymore.

Getting outside help can start with a professional assessment of the situation. We need someone who understands geriatric issues to give us an objective, neutral assessment and offer practical suggestions. It's time to educate ourselves about the condition that is affecting our parents and how this condition is affecting us as caregivers. We need to find support services for them, including home health aides or visiting nurses, and a caregivers support group for ourselves. Our caregiving goals need to include more than just maintaining the physical and mental health of our parents. We must also reduce our own stress levels and maintain our health and sanity.

Looking for alternate housing arrangements includes finding out what is available and affordable in our area. If we have a good understanding of our parents' physical needs, mental status, and personal preferences, we can do a better job of making the best arrangements for them.

## PRESENTING THE PLAN TO OUR PARENTS

Most caregivers understand that their parents will resist any change. It's unreasonable to expect that we can waltz in, sit down, present a plan, and have them say, "What a good idea." The truth is that any plan is going to be short of optimum. There are no perfect choices—youth, health, strength, and vitality are in the past. Our plan has to accommodate their marginal health, minimal strength, loss of independence, declining mental abilities, and temporary stability. There is no permanent fix. The only constant is an inexorable downhill slide.

If we have been researching the problem, then we have given the problem a great deal of thought and have weighed several options—and probably all leave much to be desired. Dan said, "Every option seemed to be a choice between lousy, crummy, bad, and poor." We didn't come to a final decision easily or lightly, and neither will our parents.

Rather than get angry and defensive, we should put ourselves in their position and be sympathetic to their feelings. We can respect their point of view by acknowledging it. To show that we heard them, we can repeat what they say. "I understand that it makes you sad to think that you might have to move to a new place." "You feel strongly that you don't want a stranger in the house taking care of you."

We can describe the services we have in mind. We can explain in detail how it will work, including who, how often, what it will cost. Where possible, we can try to show that the service will help them stay independent a bit longer. "It's hard for you to push a vacuum cleaner and mop the floors, so a cleaning service will help you keep a neat and clean house. They will even do your laundry so you won't have to carry clothes up and down the stairs anymore."

We can ask our parents to help us by accepting this service. "I won't have to worry as long as someone is with you." "I'll have time to sit and talk if someone else comes in to give you a bath."

Money, or lack thereof, is a handy excuse for many parents. Even when funds are limited, "I can't afford it" might really mean "I don't want to spend my money this way." Sometimes we can offer the service as a gift for a birthday or holiday. Once the service is established, we can quietly transfer payment responsibility back to our parents. If our parents need but cannot afford the service, we will have to investigate county or state aid to find out what services they are eligible for.

Whenever possible, it will help to have a healthcare professional, doctor, clergyperson, social worker, or other appropriate authority figure present the plan and make any recommendations. In most cases, it is better if we are present. Then we can say, "I have to agree with _____. He/she is a professional, so I trust his/her advice."

This is another instance when old family arguments are likely to flare up. To minimize this, we may want to meet with our siblings before presenting any plan to our parents. It might be a good idea to include healthcare professionals at this meeting too. We may not be able to avoid a heated argument, but we can be confident we're at least moving toward resolution.

We can also learn not to take our parents' reactions personally when they direct their anger at us or when they reject our plan. Instead we can step away from an emotional reaction by understanding that our parents are rejecting aging, not us.

# TEN

## TAKING CARE OF THE CAREGIVERS

Caregivers need to face this fact: If we don't take care of ourselves, we won't be able to care for anyone else. We may be putting most of our time and energy into caring for our parents and not doing anything to take care of ourselves. Most caregivers learn this the hard way—we run ourselves ragged, get sick, break down, collapse. The day comes when we fall apart and can't put ourselves back together. Only then does it occur to us that maybe we need some rest and recuperation time too. In some cases, we may have become so ill that continuing to care for our parents is no longer an option for us.

Marjory said, "I was run down and tired, but I'd think, so is everybody else. It was a real shock when I ended up in the hospital. Yet now that I look back on it, the signs were there all along. My body was talking, but I wasn't listening."

We're quick to respect the needs of our parents, but most of the time we barely acknowledge, much less respect, our own needs. Imagine a teeter-totter with us, the caregivers, on one end of the board and our aging parents on the other end. As the needs of our parents increase, their end of the board gets heavier. Our stress increases too, but we ignore those symptoms and let the balance shift toward our parents. If the board is to become balanced again, we have to take care of ourselves because our needs as caregivers have increased equally with our parents' needs. Now we have to look at caregiving in a new way—finding a balance between their needs and our own.

Every time we ask a question about our parents, we should ask the same question about ourselves. What is the best exercise for Mom? What is the best exercise for us? Does Dad need a special diet? Do we need a special diet? When is Mom's next physical checkup? When is ours?

## BURNOUT

Whether our parents live nearby or across the country, the caregiving burden is enormous. We are naive about how involved we'll be, especially in the beginning, and we are ignorant of the toll that caregiving will exact. If our family was dysfunctional, we may have poor self-care and stress management skills. Perhaps we were taught to deny, enable, or rescue rather than acknowledge our own needs.

Joyce said, "I got so involved with my parents that my husband started complaining about not having a wife. The kids were whiny and fighting with each other, but I didn't have any energy to deal with them. It was like everyone was being displaced by my parents."

Gail said, "My mother is just plain mean, to be perfectly honest, and that makes it so hard to take care of her. I once asked my dad why he didn't stand up for me, and he said, 'If she's mad at you, then she's not mad at me.'"

With our hearts in the right place, we go the extra mile to help our parents, more than willing to make some temporary sacrifices. We begin to shift our focus to accommodate their ever-increasing needs, and before we realize what happened, temporary sacrifices became permanent ones. There is no more time or room or energy for anyone else's needs. Caregiving has taken over our lives.

Holly said, "My parents had moved closer to me because they were getting older. Everything was fine for the first couple of years, and then my dad had to have open-heart surgery. Two months later, we went through the same thing with my mother. There was a nurse with them for a few weeks to help out, but mostly it was me sleeping on their sofa all winter while my husband took over for our three boys."

We become much more emotional. We cry more easily, we are more irritable, we feel depressed, inadequate, and guilty. We're secretly ashamed because we must not be doing enough. Some of us become overly busy, running from chore to chore without assigning priorities to the tasks or our time. Other caregivers tend to withdraw and isolate, turning down invitations with friends, dropping out of the social scene. We may become resentful that others are having fun when we are not.

We start to gain weight or lose weight because we are not eating properly. We're tired because we're not exercising, and we're sleep deprived. We're having trouble with our job. We're arguing with our spouse, snapping at our children.

We're burned out because we're taking care of everybody but ourselves.

In some cases, burnout can go to an extreme, leading to elder abuse, a hidden response to the stresses of caregiving. We become physically abusive, handling our parents roughly, hitting them. We become emotionally abusive, accusing our parents of ruining our lives, calling them names, yelling at them. We become neglectful, leaving them alone for hours at a time, ignoring their pleas for help, forgetting to feed them, refusing to clean them. If we've become this burned out, we need to get help immediately. Regardless of how difficult the caregiving is, no matter how demanding our parents are, abuse is never acceptable.

### SELF-PITY

Caregiving is a fertile breeding ground for self-pity. We are sometimes accused of being martyrs, often with considerable justification. We feel like we're doing more than our share, and we're careful to let everybody know. We feel that no one appreciates what we do, so we complain loudly to anyone within earshot.

We say, "Look what they've done to me." "I'm this way because of my terrible childhood." "They just don't care about me or they wouldn't do that." "I do all the giving and get nothing in return." "Why does this always happen to me?" "No one knows how I have suffered." "I'm not getting what I deserve." "I only want what's fair." "I'm too busy to do anything I'd like." "I guess I'll have to do this by myself." "No one listens to me." "No one cares."

We start to believe that other people or external circumstances determine what happens to us as caregivers. We look for a person or situation to blame when the caregiving becomes difficult and seemingly impossible. We struggle to explain our distress, searching for a reason that will vindicate the way we feel. We become so insufferable that other family members say, "It can't be that bad. You wanted to do this. Leave us alone."

If we want change to occur, it has to come from us. The only change possible is the way we react. The external circumstances will not change. Our parents and other family members will not change. Our caregiving responsibilities will not be lifted magically. Only our personal response to caregiving can change.

The anxiety we experience is certainly real. Caregiving is hard. We are frightened by the responsibility and overwhelmed by our parents' demands. There may have been no caregiving models to guide us. We don't know what caregivers are supposed to do or how we should feel. We're doubtful that we can endure much more.

We can learn new ways to handle the stresses of caregiving, however. We can look for help outside our family of origin. We can learn to respond to each crisis as an opportunity to learn something new. We can accept that caregiving is a fact of our lives, that no one is to blame, and that we may be the ones needing care in the future.

### SETTING BOUNDARIES

It is not uncommon to have two sets of parents ill and needy at the same time. Marilyn said, "My in-laws lived in the next block; my parents lived in the next state. They were all ailing at the same time, and it was obvious no one was going to get better."

It is up to us to decide what we can and want to do for our parents. We must set our own caregiving standards as to what is possible and reasonable. These are the values that are in our hearts, the values that will make it possible for us to look at ourselves in the mirror one day and say, "We did what was right; we did a good job."

We have to remember that it makes no difference what another caregiver does or does not do. It doesn't matter what the rest of the world thinks. It's our conscience that counts. It's up to us to decide whether we want to help our parents once a day or never. Suzanne takes her mother shopping every other Friday; Matt visits his parents every two months; Lori phones her mother every day; Marianne insisted her father live with her.

We have to decide what our caregiving limits and boundaries are. We must understand that as caregivers, we will get little or no approval for our choices. These boundaries are ours, and no one else's. If our parents will not honor them, we must.

Camille said, "I kept getting myself in the same bind. I'd say to my parents, 'These are my limits,' and of course, they wouldn't like that. Then I'd think, 'Gee, if my parents don't approve, I must be wrong,' so I'd give into their demands. Then I'd hate myself because deep down I knew I wasn't being unreasonable. They were."

Some of us may need to accept that our parents will never give us the approval we want. As a result, we defend and explain and look for approval when we're unsure. We say we want to convince our brother or uncle or mother, but we're really trying to convince ourselves.

When we're comfortable with what we're doing, we no longer need to justify our actions. When our parents complain, we acknowledge their point of view. We respect that they chose their reactions. We did not cause it and we cannot change it.

We say, "I know you want me to visit more often" or "I can see that you're upset." We quietly walk away when another's behavior is inappropriate, saying, "I have to leave when you yell at me" or, "I will talk to you tomorrow when you're sober."

We can be clear about our intentions with other family members. Greg's brother called to talk about selling their mother's house. "He was in a lather about how much work had to be done. Finally I said very quietly, 'You don't have to push me. I'm always there when I'm needed.' I didn't raise my voice, but it sure stopped his complaining."

Sometimes caregivers need to remind themselves of the big picture, one that can be very sad. The truth is, we are going to lose our parents. Between now and then, we are not going to make the situation much better, nor are we going to make it much worse. Still, we take care of our parents because it is an opportunity to resolve old issues. It's our chance to make peace with them at long last. If we do this work, we can remember their last years with a clear conscience.

## FINDING A THERAPIST

One of the most important sources of support for caregivers is a therapist. Taking care of our parents brings up old family issues that are best addressed with the help of a professional. A therapist is not a magic fix-it person. A therapist is a companion on our caregiving journey, someone who will be there for us. A therapist can help us learn about dysfunctional families, remove roadblocks in our thinking, give us needed perspective, teach us about boundaries, and offer ways to deal effectively with our parents and other family members. A therapist will help us to discover our own limits. If we can't overcome our anger and resentment, if we have been hurt so badly that we can't give back, if we are at risk for harming our parents, we will need a therapist to help us come to terms with our caregiving limitations. We may even decide that it would be unfair to our parents if we were to be their primary caregiver. It is important to develop a good rapport with our therapist, a relationship based on trust and concern. We can begin by asking therapists what their credentials are. A sign outside of the door that reads "family therapist" does not constitute professional training. We're entitled to be sure we're dealing with a licensed clinical social worker, psychiatrist, or a psychologist with a Ph.D. or Psy.D. degree.

It is okay to request an interview with the therapist that we are considering. We can begin with family issues that we are familiar with and ask about the therapist's experience in dealing with these problems. For example, "I am aware that several members of my immediate family have had problems with alcohol. What is your training in this area? Have you had other clients with these issues?"

We need to pay attention to how the therapist responds. The response should be about us, not the therapist. Good therapists are good listeners. They may not agree with us, but they will make us feel like we are being heard. They will respond to our story, our issues, not their own. Most important, they will help us turn the problems of caregiving into the process of healing.

## SUPPORT GROUPS

Caregiver support groups can be invaluable resources for practical information and assistance. These support groups usually have a qualified leader, typically a social worker. Organizations that deal with aging seniors, such as hospitals or adult day care centers, often sponsor caregiver support groups. Many groups present information on one topic each month, for example, preventing falls in the home or exercise for seniors or how to evaluate a nursing home. The goal is to inform members and let them share their experiences on that issue.

There are support groups for specific diseases, such as cancer, strokes, or dementia. The more we educate ourselves about a specific disease, the more we can understand how to deal with it. We learn what to expect, what we have ahead of us. The prognosis may not be as hopeful as we'd like, but it won't be surprising.

If we are in recovery from drug or alcohol abuse, we may at times feel that the stressors of caregiving could threaten our sobriety. If that's the case, we need to attend, or continue to attend, support groups such as Alcoholics Anonymous or Narcotics Anonymous. These support groups acknowledge family dysfunctions and keep us from relapsing. They help us remember that nothing is as bad as when we were using. These are the groups that first showed us it is possible to deal with problems while we're sober, that we no longer need to escape into a haze of drugs and alcohol. These are the groups that helped us find ourselves, and we should return as often as we need in order to maintain our sobriety in spite of the stress of the caregiving years.

Support groups offer a perspective that most caregivers need. We learn that we're not alone, that other families are dealing with these problems too. We can talk freely about the problems we're facing without hurting anyone's feelings. We discover that our fears and emotions are normal and part of the caregiving process. We discover new tools, innovative so-lutions, and new ways to approach the old problems. Listen-ing to other caregivers helps us realize that our situation is neither bad nor good. It has been better, and it probably will get worse, but today it is what it is.

## FRIENDS

Our friends can be wonderful sources of support, especially when communication among family members is strained. As our duties continue and caregiving takes up more and more of our energy, however, we may find that we're pushing our friends away. We plead that we have no time to chat or relax, and the intensity of our emotions puts them off. We obsess about family issues and burnout and terminal illnesses, but not everyone is ready to confront these issues.

We should take care to respect our friends' boundaries. They are not our therapists, so we should not burden them with our family issues. Our friends can't fix our lives, nor should we expect them to try. They may not agree with us or even understand why we feel the way we do, but our true friends will stand by us anyway. They want to help us because they can see that we're tired and hurting, but they may not know what to do. We can tell them we need to have fun.

Francine said, "Three girlfriends dragged me away for a weekend of early Christmas shopping. It was two days of nonstop talking and nibbling and staying up late and laughing. It was just what I needed."

Nancy said, "I was exhausted from all the caregiving, and my friend suggested that we take an aerobics class together. She had to talk me into it, and I certainly never would have signed up on my own, but it was a big turning point for me. It was so much fun and I felt so much better that I was afraid to stop. We've been exercising together every Monday, Wednesday, and Friday morning for almost ten years now."

### PHYSICAL RESPONSES TO STRESS

When we are living with stress, we are bathing ourselves in stress hormones. If we are to stay healthy—and we must, if we are to be of any help to our aging parents—then we need to let our bodies heal from the constant turmoil. We're going to have to learn how to take care of ourselves. The surprise is, we can, and with very little time and effort.

The process of aging causes stress for both the parent and the caregiver. Yet the stress on the caregiver is usually overlooked because the needs of the parent are so much more obvious. It is not only the caregiver who is under stress. It is the family and friends of the caregiver. It is the other people in the circle of care.

Stress is our reaction to an event. Our reaction can be physical or emotional, positive or negative. Positive stress is what adds spark and spice to our lives, just as tension on a violin string is necessary for a beautiful musical sound.

Our bodies will respond to stress in predictable ways. When we are under stress, all of our senses are heightened. We are more aware. Our skin crawls. Our eyes dart from side to side. Our hearing is temporarily more acute. Our heart starts to race. Our pulse and blood pressure increase. We begin to breathe more quickly but with more shallow breaths. In extreme stress, we start to hyperventilate.

Constant stress lowers our immune resistance and increases our tendency toward brittle bones. When we are under stress, our body produces more cortisol. The extra chemical released in our bodies increases the likelihood of gastrointestinal problems. Our thyroid speeds up and we feel a little jittery. We get tired more easily because our metabolism has revved up, and in some cases, we start to lose weight.

Under stress, we use up our endorphins, so we become more agitated, more easily depressed, more sensitive to pain. We do not produce as many sex hormones, so our sex drive decreases. Our digestive tract will start to shut down. We have a dry mouth; we will urinate and defecate more frequently. We put out more insulin and no longer metabolize blood sugar as well, so we have an increased tendency toward diabetes. Our cholesterol increases, leading to more plaque within our arteries, which increases our chances of stroke and heart disease.

Our bodies are lightning rods for stress, if only we pay attention. Too often, we ignore the signals. We don't want to be self-pitying or overly dramatic, especially when our parents are so much worse, so clearly ill and debilitated. We may start to disregard our own needs or maybe we have a lifelong pattern of ignoring our own signals, believing that we'll just have to handle it.

If we are to stay healthy, we need to let our bodies heal from the constant stress and turmoil around us. Physical exercise, mental meditation, emotional support, and fueling our bodies with proper nutrition are the keys to reducing stress and maintaining our health.

### EXERCISE

Exercise is perhaps the single, most beneficial thing we can do for ourselves. It is also the easiest—all we have to do is get off the sofa and take a walk. When we're caregivers, we don't have the energy to compute calories burned or distance covered or speed traveled. We just need to get outside and walk for half an hour.

Walking for half an hour is reasonable. We've got that much time—all we have to do is give up one TV program. We just walk away from our starting point for fifteen minutes, then turn around and head back. As our conditioning improves, we'll cover more distance in the same amount of time.

Exercise means we walk every day, rain or shine. If it's raining, we can take an umbrella. If it's snowing, we can bundle up with boots and stocking cap. We can walk alone or find a dependable walking buddy, perhaps someone at work or in our neighborhood.

We know that at least thirty minutes of exercise is best. We can break it up, but let's not fool ourselves. Those three trips from the basement to the upstairs bedrooms took a couple of minutes at most, no more. We need to be honest and put forth a little effort.

Effort means "perceived exertion." On a scale of one to ten, where ten equals exhaustion, we should try to walk at a level six or seven. We'll be able to sing a song or carry on a conversation without gasping for breath. All we have to do is listen to our body. It will tell us what we need to know. Studies have shown that we can judge our body's exertion level with nearly as much accuracy as any monitors that are glued to our chests.

Walking requires no special equipment other than comfortable clothes and a pair of sneakers. Walking also covers all the bases that the exercise gurus recommend. Walking is weight-bearing exercise. Walking revs up our metabolism. Walking exercises our biggest muscle groups—our butts and thighs. Walking strengthens our heart and lungs and gets the blood moving. Walking helps us lose weight. Walking helps us purge our bodies of toxins.

Walking alone has the benefit of getting us away from everyone. It's a chance to make some plans, figure out the next step, and review our options. It's a time with no interruptions, so we can be alone with our thoughts. We can think about something; we can think about nothing. The cobwebs begin to disappear from our minds, and eventually we find ourselves solidly in the present moment.

When we let our minds be still, we will discover freedom and peace. Then we can listen to the sound of our boots on the snow. We can smell damp soil in the rain. We can spy a garter snake sunning itself on a rock. We can simply be.

It doesn't make any difference where or when we walk; we just have to do it every day. We can walk in the morning before the household is up and about. We can walk on our lunch break. We can walk before the kids get home from school. We can give up one TV program and walk in the evening.

Once we start walking regularly, we'll start feeling better about ourselves. We'll quickly realize how essential it is to our well-being, and we'll start to build it into our daily routine. Some of us may decide to join a health club or commit to a more formal exercise program. Others may feel encouraged to try other physical activities. At the very least, while we're dealing with the demands of caregiving, we can take care of ourselves with a daily walk.

### LETTING OFF STEAM

The stress of caregiving is not to be underestimated. Most caregivers say that only other caregivers appreciate and understand the immense difficulty of the task.

What makes it difficult is not the occasional crisis, but the cumulative effect of ongoing caregiving. It's like water over a stone, a never-ending wearing away. It's the routine duties that are added to our lives—trips to the doctor, getting medical records, picking up prescriptions, following up on insurance claims, being our parents' advocate when they are living in a senior facility—the ongoing stream of minor frustrations. It's the tiny burst of adrenaline whenever the phone rings. It is having to consider our parents' needs for even minor decisions. "Can we leave Mom in the house by herself while we go to the movies?" "Should we invite friends to join us for Thanksgiving, or will that mean too much commotion for Dad to handle?" Our emotions are constantly triggered, and the extra anxiety and concern week in and week out take a toll.

Our emotions aren't bad. They simply are. The issue is not keeping our emotions in check but merely recognizing the intensity of our feelings so we can release them appropriately. We can also try to channel our emotions into something positive. For example, if our parents are receiving poor treatment, perhaps we can use our anger as fuel to improve conditions in nursing homes.

What we don't want to do is to fall apart in a situation where self-control would be the wiser choice. We need to be honest about how we behave when angry and stressed. If we grew up in abusive homes, if we were victims of abuse, we may be at risk to become abusers ourselves. If so, we need to know our limits, when and how to get help and support, when to call in another family member to replace us.

We need to remember that neglect is another form of elder abuse. We may not harm them physically, but neglect turns into abuse when we ignore their calls for help, when we leave them unattended for too long, when we forget to feed them, when we can no longer deal with changing their diapers, bathing them, keeping them clean.

We'll want to talk to a therapist instead of our parents about our resentment and how we get scared when we think about losing them. We can try to resolve differences with our siblings over the phone rather than over the holiday dinner table. What is inappropriate is not the intensity of the emotion but venting at the wrong place or with the wrong person.

NUTRITION

Because caregiving wears us out emotionally, we tend to let that worn-out feeling spill over into other parts of our lives. Regrettably, one of those areas is food. We eat out, drive through, and stop for pizza rather than come home and prepare a nutritious meal. We say we don't have time, but more likely, preparing a decent meal smacks of caregiving. We're gaining weight, losing weight, comforting ourselves with ice cream, chips, and chocolate. We're in a downward spiral of poor nutrition and exhaustion, so we kick ourselves into gear with sugar and caffeine. When we don't eat right, we don't feel good, yet we still avoid the kitchen.

Eating right is easy enough—all that's required is a minimal amount of planning. This is the time for quick and easy meals, not complicated gourmet extravaganzas. Most caregivers have been cooking for years, so we know what to do. The problem is, we're not doing it.

Where do we start? With pencil and paper. It will take about fifteen minutes to plan a week's worth of meals and make a grocery list. Once we've shopped, we're set for the week.

A good breakfast will keep us away from the candy machine at work. If we're packing a lunch for another family member, we can pack one for ourselves. If we did our grocery shopping, we can walk into the kitchen and have dinner on the table in half an hour.

Because we're under stress, we should check with our doctor, then consider taking a multivitamin every day along with additional supplements such as antioxidants and vitamins C and E. We need to drink lots of water—eight glasses a day—to help flush out the excess chemicals that have flooded our body tissues.

Eating right is a choice we make. Our bodies deserve good fuel. Taking care of our nutritional needs also benefits our mental state. We can choose foods that nourish us, or we can choose foods that numb the stress. We can peel an orange as quickly as we can eat ice cream from the carton. We can sit at the table while we have a bowl of oatmeal, or we can lean against the kitchen counter and inhale a doughnut. The choice is up to us.

MEDITATION

Caregivers feel harried, rushed, stressed, overwhelmed by all the things that need to be done. We're frustrated, prone to dumb mistakes, less efficient. We're overly sensitive to criticism from others, yet at the same time, we're berating ourselves for not doing enough, not solving the problem, not fixing it. We become so focused on the tasks of caregiving that we lose our sense of self. Doing becomes more important that being.

When we feel this way, we need to slow down, relax, and meditate. Many caregivers scoff at the idea until they try it. All we have to do is take several slow, deep breaths—no matter where we are, no matter what we're doing. We breathe in through the nose and out through the mouth. That's it.

Slow, deep breaths tell our body that we're okay, that we don't need any more adrenaline. Deep breathing relaxes our muscles. The tension in our face, neck, and shoulders begins to dissipate. We breathe slowly and deeply and without thinking about it, we shift our position so we're more comfortable. If we're standing, we straighten our spine, drop our shoulders, and lift our head. We center our weight on both feet equally. If we're sitting, we lean back, relax our arms, unclench our fists, and uncross our legs. Slow, deep breathing brings us back to the immediate moment we're in. We're no longer in the past or future. We are here.

If a few moments of meditation make us feel better, then fifteen minutes will do wonders. This time we can find a quiet place to be alone. We can either sit or lie down, as long as we're relaxed and comfortable. Again, we take slow, deep breaths, but we ignore our thoughts, letting them float away as though attached to a bubble. We pay attention to the sound of our breathing and nothing else. We inhale slowly, then exhale. Our breath flows through our body from head to toe. We empty our minds and find ourselves in the present moment.

Meditation leads us to mindfulness, or "conscious living." In his book *Wherever You Go, There You Are,* Jon Kabat-Zinn writes, "Mindfulness means paying attention in a particular way: on purpose, in the present moment, and nonjudgmentally." We can practice mindfulness as we go about our caregiving duties. When we are mindful, we bring our full attention to each caregiving task. We are present for our parents, rather than being resentful about the past or creating anxiety for the future.

Jody said, "My mother's fingers have turned into her palm because of a stroke, so keeping her nails trimmed is important. We have a difficult relationship, but when I'm holding her fingers and filing her nails, all that disappears. She relaxes, and I do my best to make her nails nice and smooth. It's one of those times when I know I'm doing something important for both of us."

The more we practice meditating, the more we see how it helps us as caregivers. Meditation keeps us centered, in touch with our body, our spirit, and the world. Every deep breath we take steadies us so we can take the next step in our caregiving journey.

## RECLAIMING CAREGIVERS' LIVES

Watching our parents fail is difficult. Whether it happens suddenly or slowly, the process is all about falling apart, all about dying. We're facing their death, and as a result, we're facing our own. We no longer feel invulnerable, protected, or carefree. We feel like we are shackled to their bedpost, their wheelchair, and their illness.

Beverly said, "I look back on the years my mother was in a nursing home and it was like being steeped in death."

What caregivers must do is reconnect with the world. We have to find time and space and activities that have nothing to do with our parents, nothing to do with caregiving. We have to maintain our own lives in spite of the caregiving.

Tammy said, "I am a substitute teacher, and it can be hard to find a sitter at the last minute for my mother [who lives with me]. But I try to take those jobs because I love teaching, and I need to do something for myself whenever I can."

There are many things we can do for ourselves that don't cost much money. What we need are activities that refresh us, lift our spirits, and reconnect us with life. Here are some ideas to start with:

- Take a class.
- Pursue a hobby.
- Learn to play the ukulele.
- Plan a vacation.
- Spend a weekend in the nearest big city.
- Attend a high school theatrical production or music concert.
- Go to a minor league baseball game. Munch on peanuts and Cracker Jack.
- Go to a minor league football game. Bring a tailgate picnic.
- Play Monopoly with your children.
- Invite friends over for an evening of cards.
- Start two journals—record events in one, feelings in the other.
- Plant a garden. Flowerpot gardens are fine.
- Buy a disposable camera. Take a picture of something beautiful every day.

- Prepare a gourmet meal.
- Get a job.
- Do volunteer work.
- Find an old piece of furniture. Paint it your favorite color.
- Read a comic book.
- Write your autobiography.
- List one hundred funny things, starting with a rubber chicken.
- Go to a parade.
- Work a jigsaw puzzle.

As we reclaim our lives and put aside time for ourselves, we will begin to find freedom. The freedom we seek will be in our hearts. We're free when we accept our caregiving role instead of fight it. We won't find freedom from caregiving responsibility—those obligations will continue—but we can choose to accept that responsibility willingly from now on.

We're free when we decide to get help—housekeeping, sitters, therapy, vacation—whatever help we need. We're free when we stop waiting for family members to say, "You've done enough, now it's our turn," and seek emotional support elsewhere.

We're free when we acknowledge that the situation may not improve, but we can learn to handle it better. We won't find extra hours in the day, but we can make better use of the hours we have.

We're free when we accept that our parents won't change, but we can. We can work on healing old wounds, resolving past issues, accepting our families as they are.

We're free when we decide to start taking care of ourselves.

# IV

---

# HONOR THY PARENTS

## ACCEPTANCE AND HEALING

# ELEVEN

## MAKING PEACE

After several years of caregiving, many of us may feel we're taking care of our parents with less stress than before. In spite of the problems, we're getting better at handling our caregiving duties, and we're even starting to take care of ourselves as well. We may have tackled some old issues, gaining a better understanding of how our family operates and how that affects our ability to be caregivers. Still, there could be a nagging sense in the back of our minds that there's some unfinished business.

The unfinished business is making peace with our aging parents. Making peace is not about our parents, it's about us. When we make peace with them, we free ourselves. Making peace means we're ready to let go of all the old issues that have been plaguing us for so many years. We're ready to move on, ready to forge a different relationship.

Any new relationship with our parents will be based on changes we find within our own hearts. The reality is that, in all likelihood, our parents are not going to change. They are who they are, and if we're going to make peace with them while they're alive, it has to come from us.

Making peace means we are ready to try to communicate

differently with them, willing to stay in touch with what is decent about them rather than constantly reacting to all that is so negative. We're ready to grieve for who they were and how they turned out. We're ready to grieve for ourselves, for the relationship we always wanted but never had. We're ready to let go of the bad things that happened between them and us so we can get on with our lives. Making peace means we want to heal.

## COMMUNICATING WITH OUR PARENTS

By the time we're caregivers to our parents, communication is probably a one-way street. Our parents talk, but they don't hear us. Perhaps their hearing is impaired, or they've always been self-centered, or their social skills have diminished over time. Perhaps losing control of their bodies makes them want to control whatever they can—even conversation. Whatever the reason, if there's to be any communication at all, we have to learn to listen.

In some families, there was very little communication at all. Maybe one of our parents had abandoned the family and the other was too busy to sit and talk with us. Or maybe our parents were unavailable because they were drunk or depressed or preoccupied with another person or another situation.

Caregivers who were fortunate enough to be the center of the family universe also communicated on a one-way street, except we were the ones talking and our parents were the ones listening. We told them about our imaginary friends, where it hurt, why we should share our vegetables with the dog, and on and on. When we were teenagers, we told them about the freedoms all the other kids had, what other parents did right and what they did wrong. We told them what we thought they wanted to hear and what we believed. Our conversation about ourselves never stopped until we left home, and on the occasions we dropped by, we brought them up to date with our goings-on.

We need to remember that our parents were once children too. They had a childhood, had a home, had some kind of parenting, grew up and matured. They had a life before we arrived on the scene—and they had a life of their own after we grew up. Chances are, we know very little about their lives beyond the part that includes us. In any case, we were surely too self-absorbed to hear about their lives, and what we did hear was filtered through our childhood eyes and ears.

Today our parents are elderly and ailing. We're taking care of them, but we may not be communicating very well, if at all. We'd like to clear up some old issues, bring closure to some earlier episodes, or simply learn more about the family history, yet when we talk to our parents, the conversation ends up being a repeat of the old dynamic between us, so everyone walks away frustrated and unhappy.

There is a way, however, to find a connection when we talk to our parents. We can ask them for their life stories. Then we can listen—we can listen carefully and listen quietly and then listen some more. What we may hear is a way to make peace.

## LISTENING TO OUR PARENTS

Listening is all about their lives, not ours. We should be honest with ourselves about our intentions. If we are hoping to talk about our own questions, hurts, and issues, we will get nowhere. A fulfilling dialogue isn't going to happen if we try to say how we feel or what we want or how hard it is to take care of them. If we want to get even with them or exact a quiet revenge, there will be no positive outcome.

We are fooling ourselves if we think we can sit down with

Mom or Dad and say, "Here are the things you did to me that were bad. . . . Here is your chance to ask for my forgiveness. . . ." That scenario is about retribution, not reconciliation. If that is the conversation we want, we're looking for payback, not peace.

We need to remember that everyone has a story, even our parents, and that every story is unique. Our parents may not know how to tell their story, or they may be afraid of what we'll think, or they may think we won't understand. Even if their memory has failed them, even if we suspect we're hearing more fiction than fact, it's worthwhile for us to listen.

When we listen carefully, we can hear more than their verbal communication. We can allow their words to be a window through which we can see their underlying feelings, their deepest fears, their heart's desire. If we listen carefully, we might even glimpse their souls.

Shirley noticed that her father's conversation turned more and more to religion. She said, "It began to dawn on me that he was afraid of dying. I contacted my minister and asked him to visit my father. He still sees my father on a regular basis and has helped him find comfort in his faith."

Clarice wanted her mother, who suffered from dementia, to move from her present nursing home to one that was nearby. Clarice said, "My mother talked a lot about her room, the color of her bedspread, where the table was, the curtains at the window. I realized that she was telling me about things that were familiar to her and how hard it would be for her to move. When I took her back to her nursing home, she immediately started telling everyone that I wanted her to move, but I knew she wasn't complaining. Mother was really telling her friends that I loved her and was trying to take care of her."

Most parents want to give voice to what their lives have

been. They may want to get their emotional affairs in order. Knowing that they are facing their last years, many parents will appreciate the opportunity to express these emotions by sharing events that shaped their lives.

Ralph said, "My father had been a prisoner of war during World War II. For many years, he said very little about that experience until my wife heard him mention it to a high school kid who was interviewing him. That opened the door for me to get him to talk about his wartime experiences over the next few years. Eventually he and a fellow soldier were interviewed as part of a university oral history project, and we have a copy of that tape. It's part of our family history now, and it means a lot to us."

## MAKING CONNECTIONS

When we listen to our parents' life stories, we are opening the door to possibilities, but we are also entering unknown territory. We hope we'll find new footing for a better relationship, the possibility that some of the old rifts will start to heal, but we don't know what is going to happen. There is also the possibility that we won't get from our parents what we want. If we are not well prepared, if we haven't given considerable thought to this process in advance, we are likely to set ourselves up for the same dysfunctional dynamic that happened to us as children.

We should consider first talking to a therapist about what we hope to learn from our parents. We want to make sure that we are ready to ask these questions, that we're ready to try and resolve some of our old issues with our parents. More, we need to be sure we're ready for the answers that we may—or may not—get.

After we have talked to our parents and listened to their

stories, we will most likely have new material to help us look at them in a new light. Chances are, the information we obtain from our parents is going to trigger some old issues for us. We will need to have a support system in place—therapist, spouse, counselor, trusted friend—to help us process what we discover. As we learn more about their lives, we stand to gain a better understanding of their relationship with us. We may even begin to feel genuine compassion for them, as we listen to what they endured, obstacles they overcame, and hurdles that were forever in their way.

### INTERVIEWING OUR PARENTS

We can begin by saying to our parents, "I would really like to know more about your life. Are you willing to tell me?" We need to reassure them that we want to learn about them, that we want the facts of their lives, and that we are there to listen.

It will be easier to remain neutral if we focus on facts. We can tell our parents that we want details about their history so that we can pass it on to their grandchildren. At the same time, we should understand that facts are also doors that open to larger family issues.

It is important that we ask only open-ended, gentle questions. We want to explore rather than probe. "What do remember about your school days?" "Which sibling did you play with the most?"

If we start to probe, we may be invading territory that our parents feel is none of our business. "Is it true that you were in jail once?" "Was Grandma an alcoholic?" "Why did you keep us girls away from Uncle Bill?" Intrusive questions can cause our parents to tell us what they think we want to hear, or they may avoid the subject altogether if they think we won't approve. If they want to protect us by keeping information to themselves, we must respect their choice.

Asking invasive questions might also annoy them enough to tell us things that will challenge us. "We really wanted a girl instead of another boy." "Your dad is not your biological father, but he doesn't know that, so don't you go telling him." "You were a mistake."

It is important that we be neutral or positive in our responses. "How interesting." "That must have been hard for you." "You were good to do that." We want to acknowledge the reality of what they are telling us and be willing to accept what they have to say without being judgmental.

To get our parents talking, we can ask them to describe their childhood home. Was it a house? An apartment? Ask them to describe it, going from room to room. For example, start with the kitchen and ask about the table where the family ate. Was it square or round or rectangular? Who sat where? Who fixed breakfast? Whom did they eat breakfast with? Did they sit at the same place every night at dinner?

Their answers may offer surprising insights into our parents' lives. As they describe the physical surroundings, most parents will begin to talk about the experiences that they had in that house, in those rooms, at that kitchen table.

We can ask our parents to describe a typical day. What time did they get up? What did they do before school? Did they walk or ride a bus to school? What did they do after school—piano lessons? baseball? chores? We can ask them whether they liked those activities or whether they were required. What about homework? What were evenings like? What time did they go to bed at night? Did someone tuck them in? Did anyone read them a bedtime story? What was their favorite story?

As we listen to our parents, we will begin to get a sense of the family dynamics in our parents' childhood homes. The details they offer will give us a sense of whether our grand-parents were readily available to our parents or not. As we hear about our parents' experiences, we will better understand what values they carry, what is important to them, and why that is so.

Sometimes we can see threads that join their lives to ours. When we hear that Dad loved his Boy Scout days, we understand why he insisted that we join the Scouts too. Or we learn that Mom once got deathly sick on chocolate pie, and that's why she never made it for us. Though relatively small and minor, these kinds of connections are a positive affirmation of our relationship.

We must remember not to interact with our parents in the sense of sharing our story too. This is a time to hear their life stories, not ours. This is about trying to understand them better. We need to remind ourselves that we really don't know what our parents are going to say. We should be prepared to hear anecdotes that are surprising to us, even disturbing. As long as we are clear that our intention is to learn, not to judge, we will be able to continue listening.

### SILENCE AND RESPECT

As we listen to our parents, our minds may wander. They may speak haltingly, or slowly, or with a lot of pauses in their conversation. As they talk, we may start remembering our past experiences with them. We start thinking about ourselves, no longer listening to what they are saying. We start dwelling on the past or our minds jump to the future as we wonder what lies ahead.

If we are going to listen and hear, we need to stay with them in the present moment and keep our minds clear. The key is simple—slow, deep breaths will keep us focused on the here and now. We can do this quietly and softly so that our parents are unaware. Each breath will bring our minds back to their voice, enabling us to focus on what they are saying.

As our parents recall their lives, we need to be comfortable with periods of silence. Unfortunately, in some families silence usually meant there was tension in the air. What we want to do now is allow quiet space with no tension, space for our parents to think and travel back into their past.

Silence need not be a symptom of uneasiness. Silence also indicates that we are willing to wait and stay with them wherever their thoughts are leading. By remaining still and quiet, they see that we are not going to interrupt them. Our silence, our willingness to wait until they are ready to continue, is a sign of respect.

This time the conversation is about them, not us, not our childhood. We need to understand that this is not always easy for us. If there are too many unresolved family issues, our emotions get in the way. We're not free to listen, or worse, we're not able to respect what our parents are telling us.

When our parents are talking about their childhoods, they are also giving us a window to see their inner selves. We may be seeing a part of their lives that they have not shared with us before. By listening, we start to see their lives in a historical perspective. We realize that our parents were products of their time, their upbringing, and the social mores of the community where they grew up. If we can be objective about their history rather than sentimentalize the facts of their lives, we will begin to understand why they turned out the way they did. We begin to respect what they lived through themselves.

Connie said, "My mother was an only child, growing up

on a farm, and she used to follow the hired hand around when he did chores. He was killed, struck by lightning in a summer thunderstorm, but no one talked to her about it. She told me how she missed him and how sad she was, but nobody seemed to understand. I've often wondered whether that's why she was so afraid of being left alone and abandoned."

Kevin said, "One afternoon Dad and I were walking along the beach, and something about his childhood was mentioned and I remarked, 'It must have been hard.' That opened the floodgates, and he talked to me for hours about it. That's when I finally understood why he was so driven to be successful. His family was dirt poor and he didn't want to live that way ever again."

Blaine said, "My mother was really a daughter of the Victorian era, with all the unspoken and unwritten rules of that time. She rarely hugged us because 'that would have made [us] soft.' She had one face for her social peers and another for her children, and her husband always came first. She couldn't show love or affection, things like that, because she didn't know any better."

Arthur said, "My mom had had a terrible childhood, and she grew up without any nurturing. Her life in the old country had been very hard, so naturally she didn't know how to show affection to my brother and me. She hit us a lot, really beat me sometimes, because that's what had happened to her. She just passed on what she had been given."

### FINDING FREEDOM

Finding freedom is all about letting go—letting go of family entrapment, letting go of the ways we have boxed ourselves in with old family scripts, letting go of needing our parents' approval. It does not mean we ignore our caregiving responsibilities—far from it. Our goal is to find freedom while still meeting our responsibilities.

We will find freedom when we can add something positive to the caregiving situation. If our attention is caring rather than obligatory, if we can applaud our parents' successes instead of complaining how few there are, we start to set ourselves free. We can bring value to a situation that may still be difficult, but we no longer allow it to damage us. We find freedom when we learn to empower ourselves as caregivers rather than become partners in our parents' illnesses.

We can find freedom by practicing the power of forgiveness. Forgiveness is not about absolving our parents of harm they did, not about letting them off the hook. We forgive so we can find peace, so we can be free, so we can let go and move forward. We can forgive our parents for the past. We can forgive our parents for being old. We can forgive our parents for being difficult. We can forgive our parents for being who they always were.

Jean said, "I feel bad for my mother because she was so trapped in her own self-centeredness. Her whole world revolved around her. She lost out on the rich times that come from human relationships because she couldn't sustain those. Her life was so lacking in relationships because it always had to be her promoting her own point of view."

We find freedom when we see our parents in terms of their personal history and that they did the best they could with what they had to work with. We're free when we can see that history also applies to us, that we too have the personality we have and the parents we were given and the times we were born in. We're free when we accept that this is what we have to work with.

We find freedom when we realize how much more capable we are than our parents. Perhaps we used to be controlled by their emotional barrage, but now we are able to sidestep it and move on.

Leah said, "It was important for me to realize how much stronger I was than she. Here was an infantile, needy human being, and I had so many more strengths and I realized how much I didn't need her. It really reinforced the pathos of her life."

## GRATITUDE

Many caregivers go through periods when gratitude seems impossible. When we're emptying bedpans or changing adult diapers or holding their teeth in the palm of our hand, we'll feel many emotions, but gratitude will not be on the list. Certainly when we are in the midst of an emergency, we will have no time or energy for feeling grateful. It takes all the energy we have to simply get through the crisis.

Some crises turn out to be times when we can be grateful for having an example of what *not* to do. We can silently thank our parents for showing us what will happen if we abuse alcohol over a lifetime, or if we are morbidly obese, or if we refuse to get help for depression, or if we stay in an abusive relationship, or if we allow our debts to spiral out of control. We can be grateful that they showed us the consequences of denial.

Gratitude is a very powerful tool for making peace with our parents, and it's a tool that caregivers tend to overlook. If we're taking care of them, it's probably because there was something they did right. At the very least, simply being our parents puts a hold on our hearts that binds us to them.

Gratitude is a way of authenticating what is good about our relationship with them. Perhaps we learned how to make a perfect piecrust. Or we learned to appreciate bluegrass music. Or we learned that paying our creditors would make our lives easier than theirs had been. Perhaps we are more in-dependent and self-sufficient because of their inattention.

Nikki said, "I sent my mother a letter for Mother's Day, thanking her for the things she had done that were good and had made me happy. I'd had a very difficult relationship with her, so it was a hard letter to write. It took me a couple of weeks to think of things, but I wanted to give her something positive. I thanked her for her Prussian backbone, for giving me piano lessons, for sending me to Girl Scout camp, for teaching me the art of arranging flowers, things like that. After I sent the letter, I felt better for having done it, and I knew it didn't matter what happened. As it turned out, she called each of my kids and read the letter to them and cried. She was very touched, but she never called me."

It may be that our parents did influence others in a posi-tive way. We can be grateful for the good things they did do, even if much of it was directed to people outside the family.

Ryan said, "My mother was a high school teacher, and she was always accepting and patient where her students were concerned. I used to be upset that she wasn't that way with me, but now I don't mind. She left her mark on the world, and it was a good one."

## LETTING OURSELVES OFF THE HOOK

One of the difficult parts of being a caregiver is when we want to do more, but can't. Perhaps there isn't enough time, or other family members won't cooperate, or our parents persist in their denial. We can see there's a crisis looming, but we're hard-pressed to prevent it.

Peter said, "My dad was falling a lot, and I warned the nursing staff that he was not competent enough to ring for help. Sure enough, he got out of bed in the middle of the night, fell in the bathroom, and broke his collarbone."

Celeste said, "I could see my mother-in-law's foot was developing cellulitis, but everyone assured me it was fine. Six weeks later they had to amputate her leg. It seemed so tragic to me."

Once we have done what we can, there is nothing more we can do. At that point, it is out of our control. It doesn't matter that we've scrambled, asked questions, offered suggestions, begged our parents to listen. It doesn't matter that the situation might have been salvaged. It is not our fault. We may feel terribly guilty, thinking, *I should have ranted louder and longer. I should have roused somebody in the middle of the night. I should have done more.*

We need to remember that more interference from us might have postponed the situation, but in the end, it probably would not have made a difference. Even when we are able to intervene successfully, we have bought time, not life. No matter what we do, death is still at the end of the process.

Heidi said, "Last year, we were able to get therapy for my mother and she showed an amazing improvement. This year, the same therapy doesn't seem to be doing any good. I'm afraid the miracle bus isn't going to come around again."

There has to be a point where we, the caregivers, decide that we are ready to let go, ready to stop blaming ourselves, ready to accept the inevitable. We may think that our parents determine that point of acceptance and surrender. We say, "When they release us, we can let go." But in reality, it is the caregivers themselves who determine that point.

We are the ones to decide that we have done all that we can. Letting go doesn't mean that we ignore their needs or stop trying to get the best help available. Letting go means we accept the situation as it is.

## GRIEVING

The grief we feel as caregivers is the sorrow we feel about losing our parents. We grieve that they are slipping away, that soon they will be gone and we will be the elder members of our families. We weep as we watch our parents struggle to hold on to their independence, their dignity, their senses. We bemoan our role as caretakers, agonizing over what to do. Yet deep in our hearts and souls we know that there's only so much we can do, for the situation is destined to get worse. We're confronted by their mortality—and our own.

Grieving is also about us. We cry for ourselves, mourning a relationship we always wanted and never had. We mourn the relationship with our parents that we're never going to have. We shed tears for the struggles we've had, for the obstacles we've had to overcome, for the help we needed and didn't get. Our grieving is a process that takes a long time, one that we come back to again and again.

Elisabeth Kübler-Ross suggested that grief is a series of stages, that grief manifests itself in other emotions, including denial, anger, and bargaining, as well as tears and melancholy. Her work is important because it suggests a cycle, one with a beginning and an end. She tells us that if we experience all stages of grief, we can find acceptance within ourselves and make our peace with the idea of death.

We can apply Kübler-Ross's ideas to caregiving, recognizing that we work through emotional stages in caregiving that are similar to the stages of grief. As caregivers, we experience denial, especially when our parents first show signs of needing our help. We resent the time and energy that caregiving requires, especially when we realize that we're being better caregivers than they were parents. We bargain with the healthcare system and other family members, trying to "fix" our parents and make the situation better for everyone. We grieve as we begin to come to terms with our parents. We accept that they did the best they could, no matter how limited their parental abilities may have been. And finally we discover that it is this process of grief and acceptance that helps us find peace and healing.

One of the hallmarks of a normal family is the ability to let go of what was and accept what is. It is this letting go, this acceptance, that is an important part of working through a life event from its beginning to its end. When we can experience the event to its fullest with all its ups and downs, it becomes a complete experience for us. In a dysfunctional family, however, there are emotional blocks and restrictions. As a result, the experience is not complete. Family members become stuck in the emotionally reactive stages of a life event, unable to find their way through to healing. They are left with emotional baggage, unfinished business, a sense of unease about the situation.

Taking care of dysfunctional parents means learning to accept them for who they are, recognizing that they may be damaged goods themselves. We try to realize that they had no guidance, no tools to help themselves, much less us. Given their problems, did they do the best they could? Yes, they probably did.

Caregiving can help us become objective about our parents. As we go about our duties, we are reminded of what our parents didn't, couldn't, or wouldn't do for us. We can harbor a lifetime of resentment, or we can finally release them from having to do what they never did. We also release ourselves from the expectation that "this time will be different" because we understand that it will be the same as always. We accept that sometimes our parents will make sense, sometimes they won't, and we're prepared to go along with whatever we have right now.

Acceptance means letting go of past traumas and grieving for what went wrong. It means recalling the good things that they did for us, the sacrifices they made on our behalf, the ways they attempted to make our lives better than their own had been. For many caregivers, acceptance means coming to terms with the hardships we endured, understanding that we are probably stronger as a result and that some of those difficult times were blessings in disguise. Acceptance is when we can acknowledge everything about our parents—their failures as well as their successes. Acceptance means making peace with them at long last.

Acceptance also means there is a healing process at work. We discover that we can help our parents in ways they could not help us. We realize we are beginning to accept their dysfunctions, accept our experiences with them. We find that we can begin to let go of our past and move forward. Accepting our parents doesn't mean they will change, doesn't mean they will be grateful for our caregiving efforts. They might still be as difficult, as dysfunctional as ever.

Acceptance, however, will change us. We can choose to help our parents without expecting them to change. We no longer need to be consumed with regret, anger, and pain. We can be comfortable with the challenge of managing their care, for we know we have options after all, that we can now choose a new role within the family. We can empower ourselves by choosing to become appreciative, forgiving, caring, loving. We change because the process of taking care of them, making peace with them, is a journey of healing.

## DEATH AND DYING

When we can see that our parents are nearing the end of their lives, we need to prepare ourselves for what we may have to do. There's more to dying than deciding whether or not to "pull the plug." Dying doesn't happen like it does in the movies—there's no music, no close-ups, no poignant words of wisdom. If we have witnessed our parents decline in a long, lingering illness, we may be wounded by the knowledge that bodies can suffer so, that hanging on to each breath can require so much energy and be so difficult.

Greta described her feelings when going to the nursing home to see her mother who had been near death for several months. "If God could only make one stop on a Sunday, this would be the place."

Society doesn't prepare us for our role as caregivers. The movies offer us a world with simple problems and guaranteed solutions. The screen is full of beautiful people aging with charm and elegance, but that is not reality for most of us. Our world is populated with family members who are demented, demanding, and difficult. We're caring for people who have little wisdom to share and whose kind words are offered rarely, if at all. Death can be lurking nearby for some time, years even, before the body finally stops once and for all.

Denise said, "My mother was near death for two years. I had to fight my feelings at that point. I screened them out so I could do what I had to do. In her last year I learned how to make something from nothing. She didn't talk, so I tried to appeal to her other senses. I rubbed her back, sprayed the room with air freshener, played audio books. I was trying to make a bad situation tolerable, but it took a lot of energy. It was exhausting."

For some caregivers, the parental dysfunction will be there until the very end. Edie said, "I went to see my mother two weeks before she died. She was very ill at that point, so it was pretty grim. I helped her on and off the commode, cleaned her, rubbed lotion on her back—all the weird stuff you never thought you'd do. It was very uncomfortable for me, and it was even hard to hold her hand, but I did. I wanted her to know she wasn't alone, that I was there for her. But she was a tough one—she put my hand down, picked up the newspaper, and started reading her bridge column."

If our parents are fearful, we may feel the same way. We have to be careful to keep our emotions separate from theirs. Ed said, "My mother used dying as her big stick for forty years—'I'm going to die and it's your fault.' At the end of her life, she was terrified. After all those years of talking about it, she was getting close. That's when the melodrama really started. Her housekeeper was as over-the-top as she was. Mom would have weak spells, then she'd panic, and she and the housekeeper would cry and say their 'last good-byes' together, then call me. It was tough to pick up the phone and hear the sobbing.

"I had a hard time knowing what was real and what wasn't, so when I would get those phone calls to 'come quick,' I would first call her doctor and ask what I should look for. Then when I walked in my mother's house, I had specific symptoms to check out—pulse, temperature, breathing rate, that kind of thing—and I could be calm and make a rational decision about what was happening and whether I needed to call an ambulance or not. Without the doctor's guidance, I would have bought into her fear and anxiety every time."

As our parents weaken, caregivers are often riddled with guilt. We are very sad to think we're about to lose them, but at the same time, we want the caregiving to be over with. We're exhausted, and though we rarely admit it even to ourselves, their passing may be a welcome relief.

Cathy said, "The last few times my mother was in the hospital, I'd think, *maybe this will be the time,* then she'd recover and I'd feel relieved and guilty at the same time. I'd be relieved that she was better and guilty to have wanted her life to end."

Attending our parents' funerals does not necessarily mean we are done, that we have reached an ending where they are concerned. We may still need to grieve, to work things through, to come to terms with the relationship we had.

Peter said, "I didn't shed a tear at my mother's funeral because I really didn't like her very much. Still, over the next year at the most incongruous times, a malaise would come over me and I finally realized there had to be some kind of subconscious grieving going on."

Charlotte said, "I didn't cry at my father's funeral. It was another eight years before I could grieve for him. It took me that long to get far enough removed from my own anger to see that he was a sick guy who didn't do much, but it was the best he could."

Some caregivers find that grieving will have to come much later. Eve said, "When my mother died, my dad was a basket case. It took five of us to attend to his needs during the funeral, so there was no chance for any of us to sit back and grieve for my mother. That didn't happen until years later when we buried him."

Pamela said, "Several weeks after Mother died, we went to a memorial service for another of her friends in the nursing home. I think we needed to have a service where we could be alone. We could walk into that nursing home chapel, and for once be able to focus on our experience over the years, undistracted by the needs of our family members. That's when I knew it was really over and I could finish up my business and say good-bye."

# TWELVE

## BREAKING THE CYCLE

Caregiving has made us all too aware of the problems of aging. We owe it to our spouse and children—our future caregivers—to do what we can to make our aging process easier for them.

Our parents are the way they are due to the habits of a lifetime, but what about our habits? We need to look honestly at our own lifestyle, our own dysfunctions, choices that are shortening our lives, problems that will only get worse as we get older. It's time for us to quit smoking, give up alcohol, get our weight under control, start exercising. We can attend a Twelve Step group to help us stay clean and sober.

We can see that one aspect of getting old is "losing it." We will lose physical strength and mental agility, and we may very likely lose the ability to make good decisions for ourselves. Further, we know that the longer we defer decisions, the harder they will be. But we have the opportunity to plan for our senior years and make decisions right now while we're able. We can make the kinds of decisions that our parents didn't find time for or couldn't face. We can be responsible, even when our parents were not.

We need to ask ourselves the same questions we've been

asking our parents. Do we have health insurance? Healthcare power of attorney? Do we have a will that reflects our current wishes? Have we given any thought to how we would like our possessions divided up after we are gone? Do we have adequate finances to provide for our last years? Have we discussed the what-ifs—what if we're demented, widowed, can no longer live alone?

We can decide who in our lives is most trustworthy—perhaps our spouse, an adult child, a close friend, a trust officer at a bank. We should discuss our expectations, then set up appropriate measures for them to act on our behalf as necessary. By making these decisions now, we put our children in the position of being our advocates more than our caregivers. They can carry out our decisions, rather than have to make them themselves.

Taking care of our parents is an opportunity to break the cycle of family dysfunction. We know the steps they took that made their last years easier, and we know the steps they ignored. We know which caregiving duties were reasonable, and we know which tasks were next to impossible. We may not have planned to seek out this knowledge, but it was put on our doorstep. And with this knowledge is the responsibility to act on what we've learned.

Caregiving has opened the door for us to face some old issues with our parents and siblings. We've discovered that we can't always plug the holes, that some of the old attitudes and relationships will never change. Nonetheless, we're learning to let go and let things be. Where change might be possible, we are more open to new ideas than before, more flexible, more willing to follow up on fresh approaches to old problems.

We have learned to be caring, even when our parents were not. We've chosen to do our best for them, even when we feel that they offered us so little. We have learned that we empower ourselves when we can give what we didn't get.

We've learned that we have choices when we once thought we had none. Those choices may be limited and far from ideal, but there are still choices. In every situation, we always can choose how we're going to respond.

We have learned that we can do more hands-on care-giving than we thought we could, yet we admit that we can't do it all. Rather than judge other family members, we accept whatever assistance they offer, then look for help elsewhere.

We have learned that even the most difficult situations are doable. Caregiving has helped us complete the emotional stages of a major life experience, and in doing so, we step out of the rigid roles of our past. We are no longer afraid of what we feel, for we are learning that we can be overwhelmed by emotion and still cope with the problem at hand.

We discovered how important it is to concentrate on the people and events in our lives that are separate from our parents—spouse, children, job, hobbies, exercise, and more. Even when we're taking care of our parents, we can continue to nurture ourselves.

We can strive to bring grace to our own senior years. We can ready ourselves to accept our infirmities and handicaps with dignity. We can seek a spiritual path to nourish our souls. We can enrich our lives by reaching out to others. We can make peace with the people and events in our lives, let-ting go of the past so that we can enjoy today.

We can concentrate on the legacy we want to leave to our children and grandchildren. We can give them intangible gifts—the joy of reading, the satisfaction of learning, an ap-preciation of beautiful music, love, spirituality, self-confidence. We can be a role model for them, showing them that it is possible to change, to grow, and to care.

We trust the process, that events have an ebb and flow, that cycles have a beginning and an end. We have found stability and inner strength, even when we thought we would be overwhelmed by old fears. We are expanding our life skills, redefining our place in the family, and learning that we can meet the challenges of a difficult life event in a new and positive way. We have started a new cycle in our family, a cycle of compassion, commitment, and care.

# INDEX

## ABOUT THE AUTHOR

Eleanor Cade is a professional writer and editor who has worked with many leading authors and publishers in the self-help genre. She has dealt intimately with caregiving issues for the past fourteen years. *Taking Care of Parents Who Didn't Take Care of You* became possible when Cade combined her professional expertise with her work in the trenches of caregiving.